THE NM

New thinking,

new journey

Mukesh Bhati

English version

Dedicated to the direct selling industry to
which I am forever grateful

sequence

Phase-01

digital network marketing

[10 chapters]

Phase-02

Network Marketing now with Artificial Intelligence

[05 chapters]

Phase-01 Digital Network Marketing[01-10 Chapters]

- Introduction to Network Marketing
- Difference between traditional and modern networking
- Features of new generation networking

- importance of social media
- Online Networking Tools and Apps
- Digital branding and personal brand building
-

- Commonly Encountered Challenges
- Learning from Failure
- Myths related to failure

Chapter 10: The Mindset and Approach Required for Success in Network Marketing   181

- importance of positive mindset
- goal setting and planning

Phase-02 Network Marketing Now with Artificial Intelligence [11-15 Chapters]

Chapter 11: Lead Generation and Management   193

- AI based lead generation
- lead scoring
- How to reach people with the help of AI in direct selling business

Chapter 12: Customer Analytics and Behavioral

Analysis   203

- Customer Analytics
- behavior analysis

Chapter 13: Predictive Analytics and Sales Forecasting 209

- Introduction to Predictive Analytics
- Sales forecast

Chapter 14: Chatbots and Virtual Assistants   217

- chatbots
- virtual assistants

Author Introduction

Mukesh Bhati is an experienced Direct Selling professional who has made his mark in this field form last 10 years in India. With his deep experience and expertise in the direct selling business, Mukesh Bhati has scaled new heights of success in this industry and has helped many people achieve success in this field.

He has extensive knowledge of all aspects of this business, including prospecting, relationship building, marketing strategies, and sales techniques. His experience has given him the ability to understand various aspects of this industry and manage it effectively.

Writing and Contribution

Mukesh Bhati's book, which is based on Direct Selling, is the result of his deep experience and knowledge. In this book, he has presented the important aspects of direct selling business in a detailed and clear manner. His writings present business principles and practices in a format that is useful to both new and experienced professionals.

Achievements and influence

Mukesh Bhati has led many successful projects and campaigns with his expertise in the direct selling sector. Their strategies and approaches provide significant contribution to the development and growth of tho business. He has conducted many training sessions and workshops from which many professionals have successfully established their career in this field.

Personal approach

Mukesh Bhati believes that success in direct selling comes not only by adopting the right techniques and strategies but also by having a strong and positive attitude. They inspire their readers and listeners and encourage them to achieve excellence in business.

Mukesh Bhati's book is an invaluable resource to understand the landscape of direct selling business and achieve success in it. By reading this book filled with his experience and knowledge, readers can make their journey in this field even more empowered and effective.

Before being an author, he is a business consultant, motivational spokesperson and a successful entrepreneur. He inspires and informs people from lower and middle class families to realize their true potential, based on his 10 years of research, thinking and Experience has helped people to believe in themselves and move on the path of happiness, this is the author's first book as a young entrepreneur which aims to improve the thinking and working style of people around the world about direct selling industry. are

Preface

In today's digital age, the business world is constantly evolving and new tools and technologies are emerging every day. The influence of modern technologies has become even more important, especially in the field of direct selling, where personal relationships and trustful communication play an important role.

"New Ways to Success in Direct Selling with AI (Artificial Intelligence)" This book aims to help direct selling professionals take their business to new heights through the effective use of Artificial Intelligence (AI). In this book, we will learn how AI tools and techniques can make the process of direct selling easier, effective and more successful. The aim of the book is not only to introduce AI techniques but also ways to apply it successfully in the field of direct selling. Have to provide. The information and tips provided will help you improve your business strategies, increase sales, and provide an enriching customer experience.

You can use this book as a guide, which will help you properly use the powerful tools and techniques of AI and increase your chances of success in the field of direct selling.

Hope this book will play an important role in achieving your business goals and help you scale new heights of success in the world of AI.

from the author

"Success comes only to those who have the courage to chase their dreams."

Victory, a word that conveys immense energy, enthusiasm and inspiration. It is not just a destination, but a journey that testifies to our struggle, patience, and dedication. Today, we have gathered to understand the significance and characteristics of this journey.

Dear Direct Sellers, In this journey, as you strive to build and grow your network, it is important that you remain dedicated to your goals and dreams. Direct selling is a field where success is achieved only with hard work, determination and consistency.

Always remember your purpose. Your goal is not only to achieve financial freedom, but also to help others and make a difference in their lives. I believe that you all have unlimited potential. With your passion, hard work and dedication, you will not only achieve personal success but also bring positive change to your team and society.

Today, we all are on our own journey to victory. In this journey, we not only have to achieve our goals but also support each other. Remember, victory is not just a destination, it is a journey. And in this journey, every step, every effort, and every struggle is important. My best wishes to you all! Victory is waiting for you, just be ready to embrace it.

Mukesh Bhati

thank you

My heartfelt gratitude to those who have helped in making this book a reality. First of all, I would like to thank my family, who supported and encouraged me every step of the way. This would not have been possible without them. Gratitude also to all my friends and colleagues who enriched this book with their ideas and support. Their contribution has made it even better. My guru and guide, who showed me the right direction with his knowledge and experience. I will always be grateful for his support and guidance. I also express my gratitude to the readers of this book. This book would have been incomplete without your trust and support. Your feedback and suggestions are extremely valuable to me. I would like to thank my publisher, who played an important role in bringing this book to the readers. This would not have been possible without their hard work and dedication. This book is the result of your cooperation and support. I am deeply grateful to everyone and hope that this book will provide you inspiration and guidance.

Thank you!

Phase-01

digital network marketing

[Chapter 01 -10]

Chapter
01

New definition
of networking

Chapter Introduction

In the world of direct selling, the blend of traditional methods and new digital tools presents us with a new definition. In this chapter, we will understand this new definition of network marketing and learn how modern technologies and strategies are shaping the future of networking.

Introduction to Direct Selling

Direct selling, known as direct selling in Hindi, is a business model where products or services are sold directly to consumers, without any traditional retail stores. This business model has grown rapidly in the last few decades and today millions of people are associated with it. The major objective of direct selling is to provide consumers a new way of purchasing products through a personal experience. In this article we will discuss various aspects of direct selling, its history, importance, and its different types in detail.

1. History of Direct Selling

The history of direct selling is very old. This business model has been prevalent since the days when people used to sell goods door-to-door in their villages or towns. Modern direct selling began in the late 19th and early 20th centuries, when some companies formally adopted the model.

1.1 Early years

In the early stages of direct selling, salesmen would personally meet consumers and provide information about the products. This model involved direct contact between the seller and the consumer, giving the seller the opportunity to clearly explain the features and benefits of his product.

1.2 Development in the 20th century

Direct selling expanded in the 20th century, especially as large-scale companies began adopting this model. During this time, some major companies expanded globally and also made network marketing or multi-level marketing (MLM) a part of their business. These companies motivated their distributors not only to sell the product but also to add new distributors, thereby expanding the business.

1.3 Direct Selling in the 21st Century

With the advent of the Internet and digital technology in the 21st century, direct selling took a new form. Now distributors can promote their products and reach consumers through social media and other digital platforms. This has made direct selling more efficient and accessible.

2. Different types of direct selling

There are many types of direct selling, which meet the needs of different businesses and consumers. These major types include:

2.1 Single-level marketing (SLM)

In single-level marketing, sellers sell products directly to consumers and they earn commission from the sales. There is no need to connect any type of distributor network. This model is simple and straightforward, and easy to understand.

2.2 Multi-level Marketing (MLM)

In multi-level marketing or network marketing, sellers not only sell products but also add new distributors. They also earn commission from the sales of the distributors they add. This model is more complex and has more potential, but it requires more work and networking.

2.3 Party Plan

Party plan is a special type of direct selling model, in which sellers invite their friends, family or acquaintances to a social event or party and showcase the products there. This type of selling involves a social element, making the seller more likely that people will buy the product.

2.4 Catalog Selling

In catalog selling, sellers provide product catalogs to consumers, which contain a listing and description of the products. Consumers can choose products from the catalog and order through the seller. This model is simple and efficient, but it lacks personal contact.

3. Importance of Direct Selling

The importance of direct selling can be understood from different perspectives, such as for consumers, sellers, and the economy.

3.1 Importance for consumers

Direct selling is important to consumers because it provides them with an alternative and personalized way of purchasing products. Consumers can get information about products directly from the seller, giving them a better understanding about the quality and features of the product. Apart from this, consumers can also avail special offers and discounts through direct selling.

3.2 Importance for sellers

Direct selling is also important for sellers as it provides them the opportunity to operate their business independently. Sellers can work according to their own schedule and control their income. In addition, direct selling also provides networking and personal development opportunities to sellers.

3.3 Importance to the economy

Direct selling also has an important contribution to the economy. It creates employment opportunities and strengthens the local economy. In addition, direct selling also provides small and medium-sized businesses an opportunity to compete in the market.

4. Benefits of Direct Selling

Direct selling has many benefits, making it an attractive business model. These key benefits include:

4.1 Flexibility

In direct selling, sellers can control their own working hours. This flexibility provides them the opportunity to balance their business with other responsibilities.

4.2 Low capital investment

The initial capital investment in direct selling is relatively less. Sellers do not need to open a store or carry a large inventory. They can start their business at low cost.

4.3 Personal Development

Direct selling develops sellers not only financially, but also personally. They can develop important skills such as networking, communication skills, and leadership abilities.

4.4 High Income Potential

Sellers have high income potential in direct selling, especially if they are involved in multi-level marketing. The bigger their network, the more their income increases.

5. Challenges of Direct Selling

Despite the many benefits of direct selling, it also has some challenges that the seller has to face. These major challenges include:

5.1 Market competition

There is a lot of competition in direct selling. Sellers have to compete with other companies and products, which may make it difficult for them to establish their product in the market.

5.2 Lack of trust

There may be a lack of trust in direct selling among some consumers, especially in cases where product quality or service is lacking. Sellers have to put in extra effort to build this trust.

5.3 Need for continuity

To be successful in direct selling, sellers have to maintain consistency. They need to add new customers and distributors regularly so that their business can grow sustainably.

5.4 Laws and regulations

Complying with laws and regulations in the field of direct selling can be a major challenge, especially in countries where this business model is not fully understood. Sellers have to be vigilant to conduct their business in accordance with the law.

6. Successful examples of direct selling

There are many successful examples of direct selling who have achieved remarkable success by adopting this model. These major companies include:

6.1 Amway

Amway is a world famous direct selling company, offering a wide range of different products. Amway has achieved a dominant position in the global market through its strong distributor network.

6.2 Avon

Avon is another leading direct selling company, specializing in beauty and personal care products. The secret of Avon's success lies in its marketing strategy and strong customer service.

6.3 Oriflame

Oriflame is a Swedish direct selling company, known for high-quality beauty and personal care products. The company has established itself as a reputed brand globally through the quality of its products and distributor support.

7. Direct Selling in India

The history of direct selling in India is relatively new, but it is growing rapidly. In the last few decades many major direct selling companies have entered the Indian market and have achieved remarkable success.

7.1 Development of Direct Selling in India

The development of direct selling in India began in the 1990s, when some major foreign companies entered the Indian market. During this time, direct selling was seen as a new and unique business model that attracted Indian consumers. In today's time, direct selling has become an important industry in India, involving millions of people.

7.2 Indian Direct Selling Companies

Many local direct selling companies have also been established in India, which have made their mark in the market through their products and services.

These companies offer products keeping in mind the needs and preferences of Indian consumers.

7.3 Benefits of Direct Selling in India

Direct selling in India has provided employment opportunities to many people, especially those who want to operate their business independently. Apart from this, direct selling has also contributed significantly to the Indian economy.

8. Future of Direct Selling

The future of direct selling looks bright, especially as we have entered the digital age. With the advent of the Internet and social media, new opportunities have arisen for direct selling companies and sellers.

8.1 Impact of digital and social media

Direct selling sellers can now promote their products globally through digital and social media platforms. This allows them to reach more consumers and expand their business.

8.2 Emerging markets

There are many opportunities for direct selling in emerging markets as well. There is huge potential for direct selling companies in developing countries, where the consumer market is expanding rapidly.

8.3 Sustainable Practices

The future of direct selling also depends on sustainable practices. Consumers are now demanding more sustainable and eco-friendly products, which will require direct selling companies to make efforts in this direction.

9. Conclusion

Direct selling is a unique and effective business model that has seen remarkable growth over the last few decades. Its flexibility, low capital investment, and opportunities for personal growth make it an attractive option. Although there are some challenges, but with proper strategy and dedication these challenges can be converted into opportunities.

Direct selling has not only benefited consumers and sellers, but it also contributes significantly to the global economy. In the coming years, this business model will evolve further through digital technology and social media and more and more people will get the opportunity to engage with it.

Thus, Direct Selling is not only a business activity but it is a medium through which people can realize their dreams and write their own success story.

Difference between traditional and modern networking

The purpose of networking is to establish relationships with people and through them advance your business, career, or personal development. However, there are several important differences between traditional and modern networking. These differences can be seen in their methods, equipment and effectiveness.

1. Through networking

Traditional networking

- **personal meetings**: Attending conferences, seminars, trade fairs, and networking events.
- **networking groups**: Networking through various trade and professional organizations.
- **social gatherings**:Meeting people at weddings, parties, and other social occasions.
- **print media**: Use of business cards, brochures, and magazines.

modern networking

- **social media**: Networking on platforms like LinkedIn, Facebook, Twitter, Instagram.
- **Online Professional Networks**: LinkedIn groups, online forums, and professional networking sites.
- **Webinars and Online Events**: Networking through virtual meetings and webinars.
- **Email and messaging apps**: Use of email, WhatsApp, and other messaging services.

2. Networking method

Traditional networking

- **Face-to-face contact**: Building relationships through personal meeting and conversation.
- **handshake and introduction**: Establishing rapport through handshake and personal introduction.
- **dedicated time**:Making time for networking events and meetings.

- **memory and reminder**: To remember personal meetings and conversations.

modern networking

- **Digital contact**: Building connections through social media and online platforms.
- **virtual interaction**: Use of video calls, webinars, and virtual meetings.
- **24/7 availability**: Networking at any time and from any location.
- **digital tracking**: Tracking and remembering email and messaging history.

3. Benefits of networking

Traditional networking

- **personal relationship**: Face-to-face interactions create stronger personal relationships.
- **body language**: Effective communication through body language and expression.
- **immediate response**: Quick response and decisions in personal meetings.
- **social norm**: Social proof of personal networks and reputation.

modern networking

- **wide reach**: Connecting with people globally through online platforms.
- **cost effectiveness**: Saving travel and organizing costs.
- **time saving**: Time saving and instant contact through online networking.

- **effective tracking**: Tracking contacts and conversations through digital devices.

4. Challenges and limitations

Traditional networking

- **geographical boundaries**: Limited contact only at local and regional level.
- **time and cost**: Travel, organizing, and time costs.
- **limited scale**: Possible to meet only one person at a time.
- **Dependence on memory**: Difficult to remember meetings and conversations.

modern networking

- **lack of personal connection**: Lack of face-to-face meetings can weaken personal relationships.
- **digital isolation**: Danger of digital isolation from online networking.
- **Privacy and Security**: Privacy and security of data on online platforms.
- **oversaturation**: Decrease in effectiveness from too much contact and information.

conclusion

Traditional and modern networking have their own advantages and challenges. Traditional networking is helpful in building personal relationships and establishing deep contacts, while modern networking plays an important role in wider reach, cost effectiveness, and time saving. For professional and personal development, it is necessary to use both methods in the right balance. With this we can not only increase our network but also achieve our goals effectively.

Features of new generation networking in direct selling

Direct selling, also known as direct selling, is becoming an attractive career option for today's new generation. This sector, which was earlier based on traditional methods, is now scaling new heights with the use of digital and social media. In this article we will discuss in detail the features of new generation networking, which are important for the new generation in the field of direct selling.

1. Impact of digital and social media

Digital and social media have an important place in the networking of the new generation. This generation, which we can also call 'Digital Natives', heavily uses social media platforms such as Facebook, Instagram, WhatsApp and LinkedIn. Using these platforms the new generation can easily expand their network and come in direct contact with potential customers or distributors.

2. Personalization and Branding

People of the new generation understand their brand identity and personality. They know how to present themselves and their products effectively through personal branding. For this generation, it is not only important to sell a product but it is equally important to establish yourself as a brand. In the process, they also reflect their personality and ethics, which makes them stand out from the crowd.

3. Deep understanding of technology

People of the new generation are more savvy in terms of technology. They can automate and streamline their business using various tools and apps. These tools not only save time but also make the process more efficient. For example, by using CRM (Customer Relationship Management) software they can build better relationships with their customers and track their history.

4. High level of education and skills

Another key characteristic of the new generation is that they are highly educated and have a wide range of skills. Due to this they are able to understand various situations and find solutions to them. This generation continues to enhance their knowledge and skills by attending business courses, workshops, and seminars, making them even more effective in networking and selling.

5. Spirit of cooperation and teamwork

The spirit of collaboration and teamwork is given priority in the new generation networking. This generation believes that it is difficult to achieve any goal alone, and hence they emphasize teamwork. They look forward to collaborating with everyone in their network and collectively achieving goals. This approach not only strengthens their network but also strengthens their business.

6. Culture of feedback and improvement

The culture of feedback and improvement also plays an important role in the new generation networking. This generation is open and they take criticism in a positive form. They constantly take feedback from their customers and distributors and make improvements to improve their business. This quality keeps them ahead of the competition and strengthens their network.

7. Ethics and Transparency

The new generation gives great importance to ethics and transparency in direct selling. They maintain transparency in their business and deal honestly with their customers and distributors. This type of ethics gives them confidence, which is the most important factor in any business. His approach establishes long-term relationships and increases customer satisfaction levels.

8. Global Networking

The outlook of the new generation is global. They have the ability to expand their network not only locally but also internationally. Through the Internet and social media they can connect with people around the world and expand their business. This global networking provides them with more opportunities and takes their business to an international platform.

9. Micro-Influencer and Peer Marketing

Micro-influencer and peer marketing also have an important place in the new generation networking. They involve people who have small but influential followings in their social and business activities. These micro-influencers promote their products and services to their network, giving them a wide and loyal customer base.

10. Sustainability and social responsibility

Sustainability and social responsibility are also given importance in the new generation networking. They give preference to those products and services which are not harmful to the environment and beneficial to the society. This type of thinking makes them conscious of social and environmental issues and takes their business in a positive direction.

11. Innovation and adaptability

Another key feature of the new generation networking is their innovation and adaptability. They keep changing with time and look forward to new ways to operate their business. This adaptability enables them to keep pace with the changing market and capitalize on new opportunities.

12. Longevity of relationships

Another important aspect of the new generation of networking is that they emphasize on making relationships long-term. They do not just limit themselves to selling products but also strive to maintain long-term relationships with their customers and distributors. This approach not only enhances their reputation but also provides sustainability to their business.

Importance of digital integration

Digital integration plays an important role in the new definition of networking. Social media platforms such as Facebook, LinkedIn, Instagram, and Twitter have made networking global. Through these platforms, you can reach millions of people and promote your product or service.

Data-Driven Strategies

The importance of data has increased a lot in modern networking. With the help of data analytics tools, you can understand the behavior and preferences of your customers and adjust your strategies accordingly. By making data-driven decisions, you can create more effective and successful networking strategies.

personal branding

In today's competitive market, personal branding is a vital element. Establishing yourself as an expert promotes trust and credibility in your network. Through blogs, video content, and social media posts, you can share your knowledge and experience and build a strong personal brand.

AI in Network Marketing:

Using (Artificial Intelligence) technology can make business more efficient and effective. Here are some ways you can use AI technology in network marketing:

1. Lead Generation

Using AI based tools you can identify potential customers and gather information about them. AI algorithms can generate high-quality leads by analyzing data, thereby expanding your network.

2. Customer Analytics

AI technology can analyze customer behavior, preferences, and purchasing patterns. This information helps you understand which products or services to offer to which types of customers.

3. Predictive Analytics

AI can predict which customers are most likely to buy your product or service. This allows you to focus your marketing efforts in the right direction.

4. Chatbots and Virtual Assistants

Chatbots can automate customer service, providing quick and effective answers to customer questions. Virtual assistants can help agents manage their tasks, such as scheduling and reminders.

relationship building

Building long-term relationships is the key to networking success. In modern networking, it is important that you do not just focus on sales, but on building strong relationships with your customers and team members. Trust, transparency, and honesty are the foundation of these relationships.

Continuous learning and adaptation

There are constant changes in the world of marketing. New technologies, platforms, and trends keep coming. For successful network marketers, it is important to continuously learn and adapt their strategies over time. This not only increases their efficiency, but also helps them remain relevant in the market.

conclusion

Digital technologies and modern strategies have an important contribution in the new definition of networking. In this chapter we understood how there has been a change from traditional networking to modern networking and what are the characteristics of new generation networking. With this understanding, you will learn more about the use of digital platforms and their role in the next chapter.

Chapter 02

use of digital platforms

Chapter Introduction

In the digital age, the face of network marketing has completely changed. Digital platforms have made network marketing more effective and widespread. In this chapter, we will understand the importance of social media, online networking tools, and digital branding and how you can use them to promote your network marketing business.

<u>importance of social media</u>

Social media has become the most powerful tool of network marketing today. Through platforms like Facebook, Instagram, LinkedIn, and Twitter, you can reach millions of potential customers and partners. Through social media you can:

1. Wider reach: Your messages and product information can be delivered to millions of people.

2. Personal Relationship: You can communicate directly with your customers and team members.

3. Brand Building: You can strengthen your brand identity and image.

Facebook

Facebook is an ideal platform for network marketing. You can create Pages and Groups here, where you can share information about your products and communicate with potential customers. Through

Facebook Ads, you can run targeted advertisements, so that your products reach the right people.

instagram

Instagram is a visual platform, which is extremely effective for network marketing. You can share photos and videos of your products through Instagram Stories and posts. With Instagram Live, you can connect directly with your followers and answer their questions.

LinkedIn

LinkedIn is a professional networking site where you can make business connections. On LinkedIn you can present your profile as an expert and contact potential clients and partners. Sharing content on LinkedIn increases your professional identity and credibility.

Online Networking Tools and Apps: A Detailed Study

1. Introduction

The advent of the digital age has not only changed the way we work, but also how we connect with each other. Online networking tools and apps are now being used in every field, be it personal, business, or educational. These tools and apps not only connect people to each other, but also help businesses achieve their goals. In this article, we will discuss in detail the various online networking tools and apps that are currently available, and how these tools and apps are impacting our lives.

2. Importance of Online Networking Tools

To understand the importance of online networking tools and apps, we first need to understand what networking is and why it is important. The basic objective of networking is to establish relationships between people and enable them to communicate and cooperate with each other.

2.1 Networking for personal development

Online networking tools play an important role in personal development. These tools help connect us to new ideas, opportunities, and people. Be it exploring new career opportunities or exploring a new hobby, online networking platforms provide us with the opportunity to enhance our capabilities and realize our dreams.

2.2 Networking for professional development

In the business field, networking is even more important. Businesses need to connect with new customers, partners, and investors to achieve their goals. Online networking tools and apps make this process easy. These tools not only help in making new contacts but also strengthen relationships with existing contacts.

2.3 Networking in educational sector

In the educational field, online networking tools provide opportunities for students, teachers, and researchers to share knowledge and collaborate. These tools help them access the latest educational resources and information, enriching their educational experience.

3. Top Online Networking Tools and Apps

There are many tools and apps available for online networking, which are used for different purposes. Some of these major tools and apps are:

3.1 LinkedIn

LinkedIn is a professional networking platform that provides a platform for professionals to connect and advance their careers. On LinkedIn, users can create their professional profiles, connect with other professionals, and search for job opportunities.

features:

- Professional Profile: Users can add information about their experience, skills, and education.
- Networking: Users can connect and networking with other professionals.
- Job Search: Users can search for job opportunities and apply for jobs.
- LinkedIn Learning: Users can learn new skills through various online courses.

3.2 Twitter

Twitter is a microblogging platform that allows users to share ideas through short messages (tweets). Twitter is used for business networking, brand building, and gaining information about industry trends.

features:

- Tweets: Users can post short messages of up to 280 characters.
- Hashtags: Users can categorize topics and find related content using hashtags.
- Followers: Users can follow other users and view their content.
- Twitter Lists: Users can create and monitor lists based on various topics.

3.3 Facebook

Facebook is a social networking platform that allows people to connect with their friends, family, and coworkers. Additionally, Facebook is also used for business networking, marketing, and brand building.

features:

- Profile and Timeline: Users can share personal information and post on their profiles.
- Groups and Pages: Users can create and join groups and pages based on various topics.
- Facebook Marketplace: Users can buy and sell clothing, electronics, and other goods.
- Facebook Ads: Businesses can run ads to promote their products and services.

3.4 Instagram

Instagram is a photo and video sharing platform that allows users to share important events in their lives. Instagram is used for both personal and business purposes, including brand building and influencer marketing.

features:

- Posts and Stories: Users can post photos and videos and share temporary content as Stories.
- Hashtags: Users can use hashtags to categorize their posts and increase their reach.
- Instagram Business Profile: Businesses can create a business profile to promote their brand and connect with customers.
- Instagram Shop: Businesses can sell their products on Instagram.

3.5 LinkedIn

LinkedIn is a leading professional networking platform that allows users to create their professional profiles, connect with other professionals, and search for job opportunities.

features:

- Professional Profile: Users can share their experience, skills, and educational background.
- Networking: Users can connect with other professionals and view their profiles.
- Job Search: Users can search and apply for job opportunities in various companies.
- LinkedIn Learning: Users can take online courses on various topics and enhance their skills.

3.6 Zoom

Zoom is a video conferencing tool used for online meetings, webinars, and video calls. Zoom can be used for education, business, and personal use.

features:

- Video Meetings: Users can make high-quality video calls and meetings.
- Webinars: Users can host webinars and interact live with the audience.
- Screen Sharing: Users can share their screen with other participants.
- Recording: Users can record meetings and webinars and watch them later.

3.7 Slack

Slack is a communication and collaboration tool used to facilitate communication between teams and organizations. Slack is used for project management, file sharing, and chat.

features:

- Channels: Users can create and discuss channels based on various topics.
- Direct Messaging: Users can have individual or group chats.
- Integrations: Slack can integrate with other tools and apps, such as Google Drive, Trello, and Asana.
- File sharing: Users can share and comment on files on Slack.

3.8 WhatsApp Business

WhatsApp Business is a messaging app specifically designed for small businesses. It is used for business communications, customer support, and marketing.

features:

- Business Profile: Businesses can share information about their business, such as address, website, and contact information.
- Automated messaging: Users can set up automated messages, such as greetings and get-away messages.
- Quick Replies: Users can create preset replies to common questions and respond quickly.
- Labels: Users can organize chats with labels, such as new customer, payment pending, etc.

4. Benefits of Online Networking Tools and Apps

There are many benefits of online networking tools and apps, which are important for personal, business, and educational purposes.

4.1 Personal Benefits

- **New Opportunities:** Online networking tools provide new opportunities for personal growth, such as learning new skills, connecting with new people, and exploring new career options.
- **resilience:** These tools can be used anywhere and anytime, making them transcend the barriers of time and space.
- **Personal Branding:** Through online profiles and portfolios, individuals can showcase their

abilities and achievements, thereby increasing their brand value.

4.2 Business Benefits

- **Wide Network:** Businesses can create a wide network by using online networking tools, which can be beneficial to them in the form of new customers, partners, and investors.
- **Functionality:** Online communication and collaboration tools increase efficiency, improving coordination between teams and organizations.
- **innovation:** Businesses have the opportunity to become aware of new ideas and practices, allowing them to innovate their products and services.

4.3 Educational benefits

- **Knowledge Sharing:** Online networking tools help share knowledge and resources among students, teachers, and researchers.
- **Support:** These tools promote academic collaboration, encouraging participation in research and projects.
- **Diffusion of Learning:** Learning is disseminated through online courses and webinars, thereby widening the reach of education.

5. Challenges of Online Networking Tools and Apps

Despite the many benefits of online networking tools and apps, there are also some challenges that are important to understand.

5.1 Privacy and Security

Privacy and security are a major concern when using online networking tools and apps. It is essential to ensure the security of users' personal information and data, as online platforms are at risk of data theft and cyber attacks.

5.2 Time Management

Excessive use of online networking tools can become a challenge for time management. Users must manage their time effectively and avoid unnecessary distractions to maintain their productivity.

5.3 Social engineering attacks

Social engineering attacks are on the rise on online networking platforms, where cyber criminals use human psychology to obtain users' information and defraud them.

6. Conclusion

Online networking tools and apps have given a new perspective to our personal, professional, and educational lives. These tools and apps provide us with new opportunities, strengthen our relationships, and help us achieve our goals. Although there are challenges associated with their use, if used correctly and safely, these tools and apps can make our lives more successful and enriching.

The influence of online networking tools and apps continues to grow in the digital age, and we may see even more innovations and developments in these tools and apps in the times to come. In this changing world, it is important that we use these tools and apps effectively and achieve our personal and business goals.

Digital branding and personal brand building

Personal branding has become very important in the digital age. A strong personal brand not only promotes your business, but also establishes you as a trustworthy and influential person

There are many important things to keep in mind while using digital platforms in direct selling business. Correct and effective use of digital platforms not only helps in growing your business faster but also helps in building stronger relationships with your customers. Here are some important things that you can keep in mind to make your direct selling business successful:

1. Effective use of social media

Use social media platforms such as Facebook, Instagram, Twitter, and LinkedIn properly.

- **profile setup**: Make your social media profiles professional and attractive. Make sure your profile contains clear information and contact details.

- **regular posting**: Post regularly about your products, services, and business. Both timing and content of posting are important.
- **engagement**: Actively interact with your followers. Answer their questions and pay attention to their reactions.

2. Content Marketing in Direct Selling

Content marketing is an extremely important tool in direct selling that helps in attracting, engaging and retaining your customers. Through content marketing you can build a stronger relationship with your target audience by providing informative and valuable content about your products, services and brand. Let us understand in detail how content marketing can be done in direct selling and what are its main components.

1. Importance of content marketing

The main objective of content marketing is to provide valuable and relevant information to your target audience so that they feel trust and connected to your brand. In direct selling, content marketing has the following advantages:

- **brand awareness**: Effective content marketing increases your brand recognition and awareness.
- **customer education**: Helps educate customers about your products and services.
- **demonstrate expertise**: You can demonstrate expertise in your field and win the trust of your customers.

- **long term relationship**: Through quality content you can build long-term relationships with your customers.
- **lead generation**: Useful and informative content attracts your potential customers and helps in lead generation.

2. Content Marketing Strategy

Follow the following steps to create an effective content marketing strategy in direct selling:

2.1 Identification of target audience

- **Demography**: Get information about your target audience's age, gender, education, and location.
- **Interests and Preferences**: Understand their interests, preferences and problems.
- **buying behavior**: Understand their purchasing behavior and decision process.

2.2 Types of content

You can engage your audience by using different types of content. Some of these major types are as follows:

- **blog post**: Regularly post blogs that contain information related to your products, services, and industry.
- **Video**: Create videos of tutorials, demonstrations, and customer testimonials.
- **infographics**: Use infographics to make information simple and visual.

- **eBooks and Guides**: Create eBooks and guides to provide in-depth information.
- **social media post**: Post regularly on social media to keep your followers engaged.
- **Webinars and Live Sessions**: Organize webinars and live sessions to interact with your audience and solve their problems.

2.3 Content Calendar

- **regularity**: Create a regular schedule for content posting.
- **Diversity**: Create a mix of different types of content to keep your audience interested.
- **Seasonal and trending topics**: Create content on seasonal and trending topics.

3. Content Distribution

For content marketing success, it is essential that you deliver your content in the right place at the right time.

- **social media**:Share your content on Facebook, Instagram, LinkedIn, and Twitter.
- **email marketing**: Send your content through newsletters and email campaigns.
- **Advertisement**: Use paid ads so your content reaches more people.
- **Customer Community**: Create an online community for your customers where they can connect with each other and benefit from your content.

4. Measuring and optimizing content

Take the following steps to measure and optimize the success of your content marketing:

- **analytics**: Monitor the performance of your content using Google Analytics and social media insights.
- **feedback**: Get feedback from your customers and customize your content according to their needs.
- **A/B testing**: Perform A/B testing of different types of content and select the most effective content.

5. Customer Experience and Engagement

The ultimate aim of content marketing is to build a deep and lasting relationship with your customers.

- **authenticity**: Maintain authenticity and honesty in your content.
- **delivering value**: Provide real value to your customers so they can benefit from your content.
- **interactive content**: Use interactive content like quizzes, polls, and quizzes to increase your customer engagement.

conclusion

Content marketing in direct selling is a powerful tool that can play a vital role in growing your business. Through the right strategy, regularity, and quality content you can attract your target audience and build a long-term relationship with them. By following the above points, you can create an effective content marketing plan for your direct selling business and ensure the success of your business.

3. Email Marketing

Email marketing is an effective way to reach your customers and potential customers.

- **newsletter**: Send regular newsletters containing the latest news, product updates and offers from your business.
- **personal emails**: Send personalized emails to customers that make them feel you care and are connected to them.
- **automation**: Use email marketing automation to deliver the right message to the right people at the right time.

4. Advertisement and promotion

Promote your products and services through digital advertising and promotions.

- **paid ads**: Use paid ads on platforms like Facebook, Google AdWords, and Instagram. Take care of correct audience targeting.
- **Offers and Discounts**: Provide special offers and discounts from time to time. This is an effective way to attract customers.
- **remarketing**: Run remarketing campaigns to repeatedly remind your website visitors about your products.

5. Customer Service

Provide excellent customer service so that your customers remain satisfied with you and continue to avail of your services.

- **chatbots**: Use chatbots on the website so that your customers can get support 24/7.
- **customer support**: Provide proactive customer support via email, phone, and social media.
- **feedback**: Get feedback from your customers and improve your products and services taking their reactions into consideration.

6. Website and SEO

Your website is the center of your digital presence, so make it attractive and user-friendly.

- **User-friendly design**: The design of your website should be such that users can navigate easily and get the information they need quickly.
- **SEO**:Focus on search engine optimization (SEO). Use the right keywords and provide quality content so that your website can rank higher on search engines.
- **loading speed**: Make sure your website loads fast. Slow loading speed can frustrate users and they may leave your website.

7. Data Analytics

Analyze the success of your digital marketing campaigns using data analytics.

- **Tracking and Reporting**: Use Google Analytics and other tracking tools to analyze your website visitors, social media engagement, and the effectiveness of ad campaigns.
- **customer behavior**:Analyze customer behavior and adapt your marketing strategies based on their interests and preferences.

8. Cybersecurity

It is important to take care of cyber security while working on digital platforms.

- **Data protection**: Make sure your customers' data is secure. Use secure payment gateways and follow data encryption.
- **Password protection**: Use strong passwords and change them regularly. Use two-factor authentication (2FA).
- **protection from cyber attacks**: Take necessary security measures to protect against cyber attacks, such as the use of antivirus software and firewalls.

9. Rules and Regulators

It is important to follow various rules and regulations while working on digital platforms.

- **Privacy Policy**: Have a clear privacy policy on your website so your customers understand how their data is being used.
- **legal compliance**: Make sure you're complying with various legal and regulatory requirements, such as GDPR and CCPA.

conclusion

Digital platforms have given a new direction to network marketing. Through social media, online tools, and digital branding, you can make your network marketing business more effective and successful. In this chapter we understood the importance of all these techniques and tools and how by using them properly you can take your business to new heights. In the next chapter, we will discuss content marketing and the art of storytelling in detail.

Chapter 03

Content Marketing and the Art of Storytelling

Chapter Introduction

Content marketing is a vital tool for network marketing success. Effective content not only attracts potential customers but also helps keep them engaged with the brand. In this chapter, we'll learn about identifying effective content, the importance and techniques of storytelling, and content calendars and strategies.

Identifying Effective Content for Direct Selling: A Detailed Guide

Direct selling is a business model that uses a direct selling method to deliver various products and services to consumers. This involves distributors or salespeople contacting customers directly, rather than selling the product through retail stores or other traditional channels. Creating and using effective content is extremely important in direct selling, as it helps to attract customers to products, inform them and ultimately boost sales.

In this article, we will discuss in detail various aspects of identifying and creating effective content for direct selling. We'll also look at which content formats and strategies may prove most effective.

2. Role of content in direct selling

Like any marketing or sales strategy, content plays an important role in direct selling. Effective content is the medium through which distributors and salespeople reach their target customers, inform them about products and services, and motivate them to purchase.

2.1 Awareness creation

The first step to effective content is to build awareness among customers. Content tells potential customers what products or services you have and how they can be beneficial to them.

2.2 Providing interest and information

Once awareness is created, the next objective of the content is to generate interest in customers and provide them with more information. This content shares the products' features, benefits, uses, and other important information.

2.3 Building Trust and Credibility

Personal relationships with customers are important in direct selling. Effective content helps establish the trust and credibility that is essential to the sales process. Its purpose is to assure customers that they are choosing the right product and that the product is the right choice for them.

2.4 Motivating action

Ultimately, the main purpose of content is to motivate customers to take action, such as purchasing a product, signing up, or making some other type of interaction. For this, the content should be clear, concise and inspiring.

3. Identifying effective content for direct selling

Now that we understand the role of content in direct selling, let us try to understand what effective content is and how it can be identified.

3.1 Understanding target audience

The most important step in identifying effective content is understanding your target audience. It is essential to know who your potential customers are, what their needs, preferences, and behaviors are. For this you should analyze the demographic data, psychographic information, and purchasing patterns of your audience.

Example: If your product is beauty related, you need to understand who your target audience is. Are they young women who are fashion and beauty conscious, or are they mature women looking for skin care products?

3.2 Clear and engaging message

In direct selling, content should be simple, clear, and attractive. Your message should be such that customers immediately understand and get them interested in your products.

Example: If you're selling a natural product, your content should emphasize how the product is beneficial for health and doesn't contain any harmful chemicals. Express it in simple language, like: "100% natural, without any chemicals – safe and effective for your skin."

3.3 Authenticity and Reliability

Authenticity and credibility are of utmost importance in direct selling. Your content should be based on real experiences, tests, and reviews. Your customers should feel that they are getting information from a trusted source.

Example: Include reviews and testimonials from real customers in your content. If possible, use video testimonials, in which customers themselves share their experiences.

3.4 Personal Transformation

A major advantage of direct selling is that it connects with customers on a personal level. Your content should also be personalized and customized. Using customers' names, recommendations based on their past purchasing history, and personalized messaging can be helpful in this direction.

Example: If a customer has already used one of your products, your content might include a recommendation for an upgrade or a complimentary product related to that product.

3.5 Educational and informative content

An effective content in direct selling is one that not only attracts customers, but also educates them. This allows customers to make better decisions and understand the products more.

Example: If you're selling health products, your content can include health facts, scientific research, and tips.

4. Content Formats and Strategies

Various content formats and strategies can be used for direct selling. Here we will discuss some major content formats and their effectiveness.

4.1 Blogs and Articles

Blogs and articles can be used to provide detailed information to your target audience. These articles can be on the uses of your products, their benefits, and related topics.

Example: If you sell a health supplement, you can write blogs on topics like "5 Important Supplements Essential for a Healthy Lifestyle."

4.2 Social media posts

Social media platforms, such as Facebook, Instagram, and LinkedIn, can be a powerful medium for direct selling. Short and engaging posts, images, and videos can be used here.

Example: Post an exciting video for the launch of your new range of products, showcasing the key benefits of the product.

4.3 Video content

Video content can be highly effective for direct selling. Videos can feature product reviews, demos, and customer experiences.

Example: Create a video showing how your product is used and what benefits result from it.

4.4 Email Marketing

Email marketing can play an important role in direct selling. Effective email campaigns can keep customers engaged through product updates, offers, and personalized messages.

Example: Send your customers a regular newsletter that includes special offers, new product launches, and personalized tips.

4.5 Whitepapers and Case Studies

Whitepapers and case studies can be used especially for clients who are looking for more technical or detailed information. These content provide in-depth reviews of your products and real-life examples of their use.

Example: Present a case study like "Weight loss results in 6 months with regular use of our health supplements".

4.6 Webinars and Live Events

Webinars and live events provide an interactive platform in direct selling, where customers can directly ask questions about your products and get advice from experts.

Example: Host a live webinar with your top sellers to share their experiences and answer questions.

5. Effective Content Creation Strategies

So far we have understood which content formats and tools can be useful for direct selling. Now we'll look at some strategies through which you can create effective content.

5.1 Focus on target audience research

To make your content effective, first do in-depth research about your target audience. Understand their lifestyle, purchasing patterns, and their pain points so you can tailor content to their needs.

5.2 Use SEO and keyword research

Use search engine optimization (SEO) and keyword research to deliver content to online audiences. Using the right keywords will help your content rank higher in search engine results, allowing more people to see your content.

5.3 Regular updates and recycling of content

Keep updating your content regularly and keep it fresh by reusing or updating old content.

5.4 A/B Testing

Do A/B testing of different content formats and strategies to understand which format and approach is most effective with your audience.

5.5 Social Proof and User-Generated Content

Use social proof and user-generated content so that your customers feel confident that they are selecting the right product.

6. Conclusion

Identifying and creating effective content for direct selling is an ongoing process that involves understanding the target audience, creating engaging and authentic content, and using different content formats and strategies.

By properly harnessing the power of content, direct selling businesses can present their products and services more effectively, build stronger relationships with their customers, and ultimately increase their sales.

After all, creating effective content for successful direct selling is both an art and a science that must be approached with the right approach and strategy.

Importance of Storytelling in Direct Selling Business: An In-depth Study

Direct selling is a business model in which products and services are delivered directly to customers, without any middleman. The success of this business model largely depends on how strong a relationship you can build with your customers and how you motivate them. in this context, **Storytelling** The importance increases immensely. The art of storytelling not only effectively presents a product's features, but it also creates an emotional connection with customers, allowing them to see and connect with the product more vividly.

In this article, we will discuss in detail the importance of storytelling in direct selling business. We will also learn how storytelling can be used properly and how it can play a vital role in the success of a business.

1. Basic principles of storytelling

The basic principle of storytelling is that a good story connects people, inspires them, and moves them to action. Stories have always been an important part of human civilization. They animate our memories and influence our thinking and decision-making processes.

1.1 Purpose of storytelling

The primary purpose of storytelling is to present complex ideas, emotions, and messages in a simple and effective manner. A good story not only provides information to the audience, but takes them on a journey into which they find themselves and their experiences.

1.2 Impact of the story

The impact of storytelling is not limited to just the minds of the listeners, but it also touches their hearts. It creates an emotional bridge that motivates the person, makes him think, and sometimes leads him to take decisions.

2. Importance of Storytelling in Direct Selling

In the direct selling business, where personal relationships and direct contact with customers are important, the importance of storytelling becomes even greater. Storytelling can be used in a variety of ways here, such as providing information about a product, sharing customer experiences, and highlighting the values and principles behind the business.

2.1 Customer engagement and trust building

The biggest benefit of storytelling is that it creates a deeper connection with customers. When you introduce your product or service through a story, customers understand it as much more than a simple product. They see the product as an experience that can solve their problems and make their lives better.

Example: Let's say you're selling a health supplement. Instead of simply touting its benefits through facts and figures, you can tell a story where someone used the supplement and saw significant improvements in their health. This type of story not only conveys information but also creates an emotional connection, making the customer feel more confident about the product.

2.2 Highlighting the uniqueness of the product

Another important aspect of storytelling is that it helps highlight the uniqueness of your product or service. Through your story, you can show how your product is different and better than other products, and how it meets the special needs of customers.

Example: If you sell a beauty product, you can tell the story of how the product is made from natural ingredients, and how the creator behind it personally formulated it so it's best suited for customers' skin. yes.

2.3 Communicating business values

Another important use of storytelling in direct selling business is that you can communicate the values and principles of your business through it. Through a good story you can tell your customers what values your business is based on, and how it meets their needs.

Example: If your business focuses on environmental protection and sustainability, you can tell a story about how you tried to make your products environmentally friendly, and how your products help customers be environmentally responsible as well.

3. Effective Storytelling Strategies

Now that we have understood the importance of storytelling in direct selling, let us learn what strategies can be used for effective storytelling.

3.1 Truth and authenticity

The most important thing in storytelling is truth and authenticity. Customers will only believe your story if they perceive it to be true and genuine. Therefore, always tell stories based on real experiences, events, and facts.

Example: If you tell the story of a customer experience, tell it truthfully. If the customer has used your product and liked it, share the same story, without any exaggeration.

3.2 Simplicity and clarity

Always keep the story simple and clear. Avoid complex and long dialogues. The main message of the story should be clear, so that customers can easily understand and connect with it.

Example: If you tell a product story, include only the important information and present it in simple language.

3.3 Emotional appeal

Using emotional appeal is extremely important in storytelling. A good story is one that can touch the hearts of customers and motivate them to agree with what you have to say.

Example: If your story has an element of conflict and resolution, present it in a way that customers can relate to their own lives.

3.4 Focusing on customer problems

The main focus of your story should always be on the customer's problems and their needs. When customers find solutions to their problems in your story, they show more interest in your product.

Example: If your product is meant to prevent hair fall, your story could include the experience of someone who faced this problem and solved it with the help of your product.

3.5 Use of visuals and multimedia

Use visual and multimedia elements to make the story more effective. Pictures, videos, and graphics make the story come alive and better engage customers.

Example: Create a short video that tells a customer's success story, and share it on social media platforms.

4. Different formats of storytelling

Many formats can be used to tell a story in direct selling. Some of these major formats are as follows:

4.1 Customer Case Studies

Using customer case studies you can show how your product or service is able to solve customer problems. This not only gives customers confidence in your product, but also makes them understand what they can expect from your product.

Example: Create a case study that explains how a customer found a solution to a particular problem using your product.

4.2 Personal stories

Personal stories are based on the experiences of individuals who have used your product. These stories connect with customers on a personal basis and make them experience the real value of your product.

Example: Tell a personal story of how a customer made a significant change in their life with the help of your product.

Content Calendar and Strategies in Direct Selling: An In-depth Study

1. Introduction

Direct selling is a business model in which products and services are sold directly to customers, without any middlemen. A key part of the success of this model is effective marketing and content management. Content calendars and strategies are important parts of this process as they help make your marketing activities streamlined and effective.

A content calendar is a plan that determines when and how content will be created and distributed. This ensures that your content marketing efforts remain consistent and organized. Strategies specify principles and approaches that help you achieve your content goals.

In this article, we will discuss the importance of content calendars and strategies in direct selling, the creation process, and how to implement them effectively.

2. Importance of content calendar

A content calendar is part of a plan that determines what content will be published when and on which platforms. Its purpose is to streamline the management of your content and ensure that your content marketing efforts remain consistent and targeted.

2.1 Organization and planning

The biggest benefit of a content calendar is that it provides you with a well-organized plan. This helps you determine which content will be published when, allowing you to create content on time and ensure distribution.

Example: If you are about to launch a new product range, you can prepare a calendar with dates and topics for the content to be published on various social media platforms and blogs.

2.2 Maintaining uniformity

A content calendar also helps you maintain consistency. This ensures that the look and message of your content remains consistent, strengthening your brand image among customers.

Example: If you have a particular theme every month, like "Health and Freshness", you can prepare and publish all the content according to this theme.

2.3 Helpful in time management

Content calendar is also helpful in time management. It helps you set deadlines for content creation and distribution, so you can manage your team better and complete all activities on time.

Example: If you're creating content for an event, the calendar provides you with a clear roadmap for creating and distributing all relevant content before the event.

3. Process of creating a content calendar

The following steps can be followed to prepare an effective content calendar:

3.1 Identification of goals

Before creating a content calendar, it's important that you clearly identify your marketing and business goals. It's important to know what you want to achieve through your content – such as brand awareness, customer engagement, or increased sales.

Example: If your goal is to increase brand awareness, you'll include content in your calendar that reinforces your brand identity.

3.2 Identification of target audience

Your content calendar should be tailored based on the preferences and needs of the target audience. This ensures that your content is relevant and engaging for your audience.

Example: If your target audience is young professionals, the content included in your calendar should be tailored to their lifestyle and needs.

3.3 Content planning

In this step, you'll decide what type of content (e.g. blog posts, social media updates, videos) will be created and when it will be published. Also decide on which platform the content will be posted.

Example: You can create a content plan for a month that includes three blog posts a week, four social media updates, and one video.

3.4 Setting deadlines and responsibilities

Set deadlines and responsibilities for each piece of content creation and distribution in a content calendar. Ensures that all activities are completed on time and that all team members can perform their responsibilities.

Example: If you're running an email campaign, include dates for email design, copywriting, and sending in the calendar.

3.5 Tracking and Evaluation

You can also track and evaluate the effectiveness of content through a content calendar. This helps you understand what content is most successful and what needs improvement.

Example: If you are tracking the performance of a blog post, you can analyze the traffic and engagement data it gets.

4. Effective Content Strategies

To make a content calendar effective, you should focus on a few strategies. These strategies can help make your content more engaging and successful.

4.1 Diversity and Influencer Partnership

Variety makes your content interesting and engaging. Use different types of content such as blog posts, videos, infographics, and case studies. Additionally, influencer partnerships can also make your content more effective.

Example: Include a variety of content a month such as how-to videos, customer testimonials, and infographics.

4.2 Data-Based Approach

Create your content with a data-driven approach. This ensures that your content takes into account the needs and interests of your audience.

Example: Use customer surveys and analytics data to determine which topics are most relevant to your audience.

4.3 Engaging and interactive content

Engaging and interactive content engages your audience more and keeps them engaged with your brand on a deeper level. This may include quizzes, polls, and live sessions.

Example: Run a social media poll giving your audience the chance to give their opinion about your new product.

4.4 Content Repetition and Updates

Update and iterate old content regularly so that it maintains freshness and relevance. It provides your audience with the latest information and also boosts your SEO ranking.

Example: Update an old blog post and republish it with new statistics and information.

4.5 Keeping pace with trends and current events

Keep your content in sync with current trends and events. This ensures that your content remains relevant and engaging over time.

Example: Publish a fresh blog post or social media update about a major industry event or trend.

5. Tools and Resources for Content Calendar

There are various tools and resources available to effectively manage a content calendar. Some of these major tools are as follows:

5.1 Google Calendar

Google Calendar is a simple and effective tool that you can use to organize your content calendar. In this you can add dates and times of all content activities and share them with team members.

5.2 Trello

Trello is a project management tool that you can use as a content calendar. Here you can track content ideas, plans, and deadlines through various cards.

5.3 Asana

Asana is another project management tool that helps manage content calendars. Here you can track tasks, deadlines, and team responsibilities.

5.4 CoSchedule

CoSchedule is a specialized content calendar tool that helps you organize all your marketing activities in one place. This can track social media posting, blog scheduling, and email marketing.

6. Conclusion

Content calendar and strategies are of utmost importance in direct selling. A well-organized content calendar not only simplifies your content management, but it also helps make your marketing efforts effective and targeted. Additionally, effective content strategies can make your marketing even more successful.

By using content calendars and strategies properly, you can run your direct selling business in a more organized and effective manner. This ensures that your content creation and delivery is timely, and that relevant and engaging content is provided to your target audience.

By using these strategies and tools, you can make your content marketing efforts more effective, establish stronger relationships with your audience, and ensure the success of your direct selling business.In this chapter we discussed effective content. Discussed in detail about identity, importance and techniques of storytelling, and content calendar and strategies. In the next chapter, we will discuss the importance and techniques of relationship building and networking events.

Chapter 04

Chapter 4: Relationship Building and Networking Events

Chapter Introduction

Understanding the importance of relationship building and networking events is essential to achieving long-term success in network marketing. This chapter focuses on both of these aspects and will show you how you can make your network marketing business even more successful by building strong relationships and actively participating in networking events.

The art of relationship building in direct selling

To be successful in direct selling, it is not enough to just sell the product or service. Additionally, it is also extremely important to build strong and lasting relationships with customers and potential customers. The art of relationship building not only helps increase your sales, but also increases customer satisfaction and loyalty.

Let us understand the art of relationship building in direct selling and how it can be adopted effectively.

1. Understanding customer needs

- **Hear**: Listen carefully to your customers. Try to understand their problems, needs and priorities.
- **Research**: Get information about the customer's business, industry, and personal interests.
- **ask questions**: Ask open-ended questions that uncover the customer's needs and wants.

2. Authenticity and honesty

- **Truth**: Speak truthfully about your products and services. Avoid any kind of exaggeration.
- **building trust**: With honesty and transparency you can win customer trust.
- **Acknowledgment**: Take customer problems or complaints seriously and resolve them.

3. Building personal relationships

- **call by name**: Address customers by their names. It reflects personal and intimacy.
- **take care of interests**: Know the interests and likes and dislikes of the customers and give them suggestions on that basis.
- **focus on special occasions**: Send wishes to customers on their birthdays, anniversaries, and other special occasions.

4. Interview and dialogue

- **positive communication**: Make the communication positive and inspiring. It makes the customer feel excited and connected.
- **receiving feedback**:Take regular feedback from customers and make improvements based on their responses.
- **respect for time**: Respect customers' time and respond to them on time.

5. Help and Support

- **Availability**: Always be available to customers and solve their problems quickly.
- **sharing knowledge**: Share deep insights about products and services that help customers make decisions.
- **training and education**: Provide training and education to customers to properly use your products and services.

6. Maintaining regular contact

- **Newsletter and Updates**: Send regular newsletters and updates containing new information about your products and services.
- **social media interaction**: Be active on social media platforms and interact with your customers.
- **Emails and calls**: Keep in touch with your customers through emails and calls from time to time.

7. Making relationships personal

- **gifts and thanks**: Send small gifts or thank you notes to customers on special occasions.
- **customized offer**: Make customized proposals and offers based on customers' past behavior and preferences.
- **level of service**: Provide a high level of customer service that makes their experience even better.

8. Evaluating and improving relationships

- **Surveys and Analytics**: Evaluate the quality of relationships through customer satisfaction surveys and analytics.
- **periodic review**: Regularly review your relationship building strategies and make plans for improvement.
- **novelty**: Innovate your approach and strategies so that you can adapt to changing customer expectations and market conditions.

conclusion

The main objective of the art of relationship building in direct selling is to establish long-term and positive relationships with customers. This requires you to understand customer needs, act with authenticity and honesty, build personal relationships, and provide ongoing support. Maintaining regular contact and evaluating and improving relationships is also important. By adopting all these elements, you can build strong and lasting relationships in your direct selling business, thereby ensuring the success of your business.

Importance of networking events

Networking events play an important role in network marketing. These events provide you with the opportunity to meet new potential customers and partners, promote your business, and learn about the latest industry trends and technologies.

Types of Networking Events

1. **Conferences and Seminars:** These are large-scale events where you can meet industry experts and learn from their experiences.

2. **Webinars:** Held online, these events give you the opportunity to interact directly with experts and gain new insights.

3. **Workshops:** These are smaller and more focused events where you can learn specific skills and techniques.

4. Networking Meetups: Informal meetings where you can meet other network marketers and share your ideas and experiences.

Effective Networking Tips and Tricks

You can be more successful when attending networking events by keeping some effective tips and tricks in mind.

1. Preparation: Prepare before the event. Understand the event agenda and make a list of people you want to meet.

2. Go with clear objectives: Be clear about your objectives for going to the event. Do you want to find new clients, or learn from industry experts?

benefits of relationship building

Relationship building is extremely important in direct selling and other business models. Strong and positive relationships not only help in retaining customers but also play an important role in business success. Here are some of the key benefits of relationship building:

1. Customer loyalty and stability

- **loyalty**: Strong relationships increase customer loyalty. Loyal customers will use your product or services again and again and provide stability to your business.
- **repeat business**: Once customers have established a strong relationship with you, they

are more likely to repeat your products and services.

2. Positive word-of-mouth

- **reference**: Satisfied customers may recommend your business to their family, friends and colleagues, which helps in acquiring new customers.
- **brand ambassador**: Loyal customers act as ambassadors for your brand, enhancing your business's reputation.

3. High customer satisfaction

- **quality of service**: Personal and authentic relationships improve the customer experience, increasing satisfaction.
- **Solutions and Support**: Strong relationships ensure quick and effective resolution of customer problems, which increases their satisfaction.

4. Reduction of marketing costs

- **Less cost**: Repeat business from existing customers is likely to be lower cost than attracting new customers.
- **word-of-mouth marketing**: Recommendations and positive reviews from satisfied customers are a cost-effective way of marketing.

5. Increase in business opportunities

- **Cross-selling and up-selling**: Strong relationships make customers more receptive to cross-selling (recommending different products or services) and up-selling (recommending higher value products or services).
- **Feedbacks and Suggestions**: Customers share their experiences and suggestions, which are helpful in improving your business.

6. Increase in brand reputation

- **positive image**: Strong and positive relationships improve your brand's reputation and make you a trusted and respected brand in the industry.
- **customer trust**: When customers build a strong relationship with you, they trust your brand and enhance your reputation.

7. Improve market understanding

- **customer preferences**: Strong relationships help you better understand customer preferences and expectations.
- **Trends and demand**: Interacting with customers can help you gain insight into market trends and demand, allowing you to better customize your products and services.

8. Emotional connection

- **enthusiasm and inspiration**: When customers connect with you emotionally, they are excited and motivated for the success of your business.

- **brand loyalty**: Emotional connection makes customers more loyal to your brand.

9. Long term relationship

- **long relationship**: Strong relationships lead to long-term customer relationships, which are vital to the sustainability and continuity of the business.
- **investment of time**: Investing time and effort in maintaining long-term relationships pays off, as these create a permanent customer base.

conclusion

Relationship building is extremely beneficial in direct selling and other business models. This leads to customer loyalty, positive word-of-mouth, higher customer satisfaction, and increased business opportunities as well as improved brand reputation and market understanding. You need to maintain a personal and authentic connection with customers to build strong and lasting relationships, which will ensure the success of your business.

Types, Process and Importance of Networking Events

Networking events provide important opportunities to establish and strengthen business relationships. These events can be of different types and each has its own special purpose and process. Here is detailed information on the major types of networking events, their process, and importance:

Types of Networking Events

1. **Conferences and Seminars**
   - **Description**: These are organized on a large scale and focus on a particular topic or industry. These may include keynote speakers, panel discussions, and workshops.
   - **Objective**: Share knowledge, discuss the latest industry trends, and connect with experts.
   - **Example**: Technology conferences, marketing seminars.
2. **Trade Shows and Expos**
   - **Description**: In these events various companies display their products and services. It is usually in the form of an exhibition consisting of many booths and stalls.
   - **Objective**: Exhibition of products and services, contact with potential customers, and networking with other members of the industry.
   - **Example**:Entrepreneurship Expo, Hardware Trade Show.
3. **Virtual Networking Events**
   - **Description**: These events are organized on online platforms. This may include video conferencing, webinars, and virtual meetings.
   - **Objective**: Establishing contact and maintaining communication despite geographical distance.

- o **Example**: Zoom Webinars, LinkedIn Live Events.
4. **Workshops and Training Sessions**
   - o **Description**: These are organized in small groups and focus on particular skills or knowledge. The individuals participating in it usually participate actively.
   - o **Objective**: Providing skill development, education, and networking opportunities.
   - o **Example**: Sales Training Workshops, Digital Marketing Training.
5. **Social and Casual Events**
   - o **Description**: These events are less formal and held in a casual environment, such as a luncheon, dinner, or social gathering.
   - o **Objective**: Establishing personal relationships and communicating in an informal environment.
   - o **Example**: Boutique Luncheon, Anniversary Party.
6. **Business Meetings and Breakfast Meetings**
   - o **Description**: These are small and private events that involve more in-depth interactions with a specific group or individuals.
   - o **Objective**: Discussing specific business issues and building personal relationships.
   - o **Example**: C-suite meetings, networking breakfasts.
7. **Special Events and Gala Dinners**

- o **Description**: These are big and spectacular events which are attended by prominent people and influential people of the industry.
- o **Objective**: Presenting major honors and awards, and providing networking opportunities.
- o **Example**: Award Show, Gala Dinner.

Process Networking Events

1. **planning and preparation**
   - o **setting objectives**: Explain the purpose and goal of the event.
   - o **making a list**: Prepare a list of participants, organizers and potential guests.
   - o **Venue and date**: Set a suitable location and date.
2. **promotions and invitations**
   - o **promotional material**: Create brochures, social media posts, and email invitations to publicize event information.
   - o **send invitation**: Send invitations to targeted individuals and groups.
3. **Organizing and Operating**
   - o **registration**:Ensure attendee registration process.
   - o **logistics**: Arrange for the event venue, equipment, and other needs.
   - o **Operation**:Ensure timely conduct of programs and sessions during the event.
4. **Follow-up and evaluation**

- gathering feedback: Get feedback from participants and attendees.
- **Networking Follow-up**: Maintain communication with contacts and send them thank you letters.
- **Evaluation**: Evaluate the impact and successes of the event and develop improvement suggestions for the future.

Importance of networking events

1. **relationship building**: Networking events provide an opportunity to establish and strengthen personal and business relationships.
2. **Science and Updates**: Get a chance to get the latest industry trends, technologies and information.
3. **Relationships and Opportunities**: Opportunity to connect with potential customers, partners, and investors.
4. **Professional development**: New ideas, inspiration, and possibilities are exchanged which helps in business growth.
5. **brand profile**: Your brand identity and reputation gets a boost and you can present your business prominently.

Networking events play an important role in direct selling and other business sectors. These events not only provide new contacts and opportunities, but also strengthen business relationships. With proper planning, conduct, and evaluation of events, you can make your networking efforts more effective and profitable.

Common Challenges at Networking Events

Networking events also have many challenges. It is necessary to understand and overcome them.

1. Social Anxiety: Many people face social anxiety at big events. Prepare yourself to overcome this and maintain confidence.

2. Time Management: There is often a shortage of time in events. Set priorities and focus on them.

3. Maintaining Relationships: Maintaining relationships after the event can be challenging. Follow-up regularly and maintain the relationship.

Effective Networking Tips and Tricks in Direct Selling

Networking plays an important role in direct selling, as it helps in reaching potential customers of your product or service and increasing sales. Through effective networking you can connect with your target audience, establish relationships, and take your business to new heights. Here are some effective networking tips and tricks:

1. Set clear objectives and goals

Before networking, it is important that you clearly determine your networking goals and objectives. This will help you guide your networking activities in the right direction.

Example:

- **Objective:** Sharing your product information and identifying potential customers.
- **Goal:** Contacting 10 new potential leads in a month.

2. Build a strong personal brand

It is important to build a strong personal brand when networking. Your personal brand reflects your professional personality and the image of your business.

Tips:

- **Introduce Yourself:** Prepare a clear and compelling pitch about yourself that reflects the benefits of your business and your personal brand.
- **Maintain Consistency:** Keep your brand image consistent, whether it's on your professional profiles, social media accounts, or business cards.

3. Develop effective communication skills

It is important to have effective communication skills when networking. It helps you present your ideas and proposals in a clear and attractive way.

Tips:

- **Art of listening:** Listen carefully to others and understand their needs and problems.
- **Clear and Concise Communication:** Keep your message clear and concise so that the listener can easily understand it.

4. Build relationships and contacts

The main purpose of networking is to build relationships and contacts. For effective networking, you need to connect with the right people and build strong relationships.

Tips:

- **Attend networking events:** Make new contacts by attending industry events, conferences, and trade shows.
- **Follow up:** After networking events, send thank you letters or emails to your new contacts and provide them with more information about your service or product.

5. Share valuable content and information

When networking, you should make your content and information valuable and relevant. This may make your contacts more motivated to show interest in your offerings.

Tips:

- **Provide useful information:** Share useful industry tips, information, and resources that can help your contacts solve problems.
- **Special Offers and Discounts:** Offer special offers and discounts to potential customers that may entice them to try your product or service.

6. Take advantage of digital networking

By using digital platforms you can reach a wider audience and expand your network.

Tips:

- **Use Social Media:** Use social media platforms like Facebook, LinkedIn, Twitter, and Instagram to connect with your target audience.
- **Optimize LinkedIn Profile:** Make your LinkedIn profile professional and attractive so that it attracts potential contacts.

7. Collaborate with Influencers for Networking

By collaborating with influencers and key individuals you can grow your network faster and reach more people.

Tips:

- **Create Partnership:** Partner with influencers and industry experts who can promote your product or service.

- **Interviews and Guest Posts:** Conduct interviews with influencers or write guest posts on their blogs or social media.

8. Maintain regular contact

Networking isn't just a one-time effort; It is a continuous process. Keep in touch with your contacts regularly and maintain engagement with them.

Tips:

- **email newsletter:** Send your contacts regular email newsletters that include industry news, helpful tips, and special offers.
- **Maintain Relationship:** Send greetings to your contacts on important occasions in their lives (like birthdays or anniversaries).

9. Share successful networking stories

By sharing successful networking stories you can showcase your experiences and results, which can inspire your network and increase the credibility of your business.

Tips:

- **Case Studies:** Share your business success stories as case studies.
- **Customer Interview:** Interview with satisfied customers and share their experiences.

10. Analysis and Improvement

Analyze the results of networking activities and make improvements as needed. This will help you improve your strategies.

Tips:

- **performance appraisal:** Evaluate the results of your networking efforts and understand which methods are most effective.
- **Get Feedback:** Get feedback from your contacts and make improvements based on it.

conclusion

Relationship building and networking events are important elements of achieving long-term success in network marketing. In this chapter we discussed the art of relationship building, types and importance of networking events, and tips and tricks for effective networking. By building strong relationships and at networking events

By actively participating, you can take your network marketing business to new heights. In the next chapter, we will discuss lead generation and prospecting techniques in detail.

Chapter 05

Lead Generation and Prospecting Techniques

Chapter Introduction

Lead generation and prospecting are one of the most important aspects of network marketing. Correct use of these techniques can grow your business faster and attract more potential customers. In this chapter, we will discuss different methods of lead generation, effective prospecting techniques, and strategies for converting leads into customers.

Successful Lead Generation Methods for Direct Selling Business: A Comprehensive Guide

1. Purpose of Lead Generation

Direct selling is a business model in which products or services are sold directly to customers, without any middleman. Lead generation plays an important role in the success of this model. The purpose of lead generation is to identify potential customers and attract them to the sales process.

Successful lead generation strategies promote your direct selling business, increase sales, and strengthen the customer base. In this article, we will discuss the best practices for lead generation for direct selling businesses, including various strategies, tools, and practices.

2. Importance of Lead Generation

Lead generation is extremely important for any direct selling business. It is the process of attracting potential customers and adding them to your sales pipeline. It is not just a sales activity, but a business development strategy that boosts your brand identity and market share.

2.1 Sales promotion

The biggest benefit of lead generation is that it boosts your sales. By attracting the right leads, you can make contact with potential customers and inspire them to purchase your product or service.

2.2 Expanding customer base

Lead generation also expands your customer base. By attracting new leads, you can build a strong and diverse customer base for your business, ensuring your long-term success.

2.3 Increase in brand awareness

Lead generation activities also boost awareness of your brand. When you attract new leads, you provide more people with information about your brand, strengthening your brand identity.

3. Best Ways to Lead Generation

There are many methods of effective lead generation for direct selling business. By using these methods correctly, you can get more leads and convert them into sales. Here are some successful lead generation methods being discussed:

3.1 Content Marketing

Content marketing is an important and effective method for lead generation. It involves creating valuable and engaging content that attracts potential customers to you.

Example:

- **Blog Posts:** Write regular blog posts that showcase your expertise and help solve potential customers' problems.
- **eBooks and Guides:** Create eBooks and guides to provide information to potential customers and make them available for download.

Strategy:

- Optimize your content with SEO (Search Engine Optimization) so it can rank higher in search engines and reach more people.
- Promote your content on social media and include it in your email newsletter.

3.2 Social Media Marketing

Social media platforms like Facebook, Instagram, and LinkedIn are highly effective for lead generation. These platforms provide you with the opportunity to reach your target audience and connect with potential customers.

Example:

- **Facebook Ads:** Run targeted ads on Facebook that expose your product or service to potential customers.

- **LinkedIn Networking:** Expand your network on LinkedIn and establish relationships with potential leads.

Strategy:

- Update your social media profiles regularly and share engaging posts and content.
- Interact with your target audience and understand their problems and needs.

3.3 Email Marketing

Email marketing is an effective lead generation strategy that helps you maintain constant contact with your potential customers. It involves sending regular emails to your target audience containing information about your product or service.

Example:

- **Welcome Emails:** Send welcome messages to new leads and let them know the benefits of your product or service.
- **Newsletter:** Send regular email newsletters that include news, tips, and special offers related to your industry.

Strategy:

- Segment your email list so you can send personalized and targeted messages.
- Make email subject lines and content attractive so that more people open and read them.

3.4 Webinars and Online Events

Webinars and online events are effective for lead generation because they provide potential customers with more information about your product or service and give them an opportunity to engage with your business.

Example:

- **Presentations:** Conduct an online presentation about the features and benefits of your product or service.
- **Q&A Session:** Hold a Q&A session with potential customers where they can ask their questions about your product.

Strategy:

- Use social media, email, and your website to market webinars and events.
- Partner with partners and influencers to expand the reach of your events.

3.5 Referral Programs

Referral programs encourage your existing customers to attract new customers to your business. This is a powerful method because it is based on recommendations from existing customers, which generally brings in high quality leads.

Example:

- **Incentives:** Offer special discounts or gifts to your existing customers to bring in new leads.
- **Referral Link:** Provide a referral link that customers can share with their networks.

Strategy:

- Promote your referral program clearly and explain how your customers can benefit.
- Track referral program results and make adjustments as needed.

3.6 Networking and Partnerships

Networking and partnerships can be an effective method for lead generation as they give you the opportunity to contact new potential customers and discover new opportunities.

Example:

- **Industry Events:** Attend industry conferences and trade fairs so you can meet with potential customers and partners.
- **Sharing:** Partner with other businesses and influencers who can reach your target audience.

Strategy:

- Actively participate in networking events and interact effectively.
- Communicate regularly with potential partners to establish relationships and explore collaboration opportunities.

4. Useful Tools for Lead Generation

Many tools and software help make lead generation simpler and more effective. Here is a list of some of the major tools:

4.1 CRM Software (Customer Relationship Management)

CRM software helps you track, manage, and improve communication with your leads.

Example:

- **Salesforce:** A leading CRM tool for lead tracking and sales pipeline management.
- **HubSpot:** An all-in-one CRM and marketing automation platform.

4.2 Lead Generation Tools

Lead generation tools simplify the process of capturing and managing leads on your website.

Example:

- **OptinMonster:** A tool for creating lead capture forms and pop-ups.
- **Leadpages:** A tool for lead capture page and landing page creation.

4.3 Email Marketing Software

Email marketing software helps you create, send, and track email campaigns.

Example:

- **Mailchimp:** A popular software for creating and tracking email campaigns.
- **Constant Contact:** A tool for email marketing and lead management.

4.4 Social Media Analytics Tools

Social media analytics tools help you track and measure the success of your social media activities.

Example:

- **Hootsuite:** A tool for social media management and analytics.
- **Sprout Social:** A platform for social media intelligence and analytics.

5. Conclusion

Lead generation plays an important role in direct selling business. There are various strategies and tools available for successful lead generation, which can make your marketing efforts more effective. Strategies like content marketing, social media marketing, email marketing, webinars, referral programs, and networking can help you get more leads and convert them into sales.

Tools like content calendars, CRM software, lead generation tools, and social media analytics tools can make your lead generation process streamlined and effective. By using these methods and tools properly, you can boost the success of your direct selling business and build a strong customer base.

Prospecting techniques in modern era direct selling

Prospecting is an important stage of direct selling which involves the process of identifying potential customers and attracting them to make a sale. In the modern era, technology and digital tools have changed the methods of prospecting to a great extent. Let us know what are the major techniques of prospecting in modern direct selling:

1. Social Media Prospecting

- **use of social platforms**: Identify and communicate with potential customers on social media platforms like Facebook, LinkedIn, Instagram, and Twitter.
- **Communities and Groups**: Be active in groups and communities related to your related industry or interests and promote your services or products.
- **targeted advertising**: Run targeted ads on social media that help you reach your target audience.

2. Digital Marketing and Content Marketing

- **Blogging and Articles**: Write blog posts and articles related to your industry that showcase your expertise and attract potential clients.
- **eBooks and Guides**: Create informative e-books and guides and make them available for download to increase your lead generation.
- **video content**: Create product demonstrations, customer testimonials, and tutorial videos and share them on your website and social media channels.

3. Email Marketing

- **email newsletter**: Send regular email newsletters containing information related to your products, services, and industry.
- **personalized emails**: Send personalized emails to prospects that are tailored to their specific needs and preferences.
- **Lead Nurturing**: Use automated email sequences that provide potential customers with more information about your products and services and inspire them to make a purchase.

4. Data Analytics and CRM

- **data analysis**: Use data analytics to understand the behavior and preferences of potential customers.
- **CRM software**: Track and manage potential customer information and interactions using customer relationship management (CRM) software.
- **lead scoring**: Score leads so you can focus more on those with the most potential.

5. Networking and Referrals

- **networking events**: Attend industry-related networking events, conferences, and seminars and make new contacts.
- **Referral Programs**: Offer incentives to get referrals from your existing customers and help them reach out to your potential customers.

6. Online Advertising and SEO

- **paid advertising**: Use Google AdWords, Facebook Ads, and other paid advertising channels that provide direct access to your target audience.
- **Search Engine Optimization (SEO)**: Optimize your website according to SEO best practices so that potential customers can easily access your site and get information about your offerings.

7. Smartphones and mobile apps

- **mobile marketing**: Target potential customers through SMS and mobile notifications.
- **mobile apps**: Build mobile apps to provide information about your services and products in a way that is convenient for users.

8. Online Surveys and Feedback

- **survey**: Collect online surveys and feedback from potential customers so you can understand their needs and wants.
- **customer feedback**: Collect feedback from existing customers and use the information to attract new customers.

9. Virtual Meetings and Webinars

- **Webinars**: Organize webinars by industry experts and invite potential customers so they can learn more about your products and services.
- **virtual meetings**: Communicate directly with potential customers through virtual meetings and answer their questions.

conclusion

In the modern era, the techniques of prospecting in direct selling are continuously evolving. By using social media, digital marketing, email marketing, data analytics, and other digital tools, you can easily reach potential customers and attract them to your products and services. Using these techniques properly can make your prospecting process more effective and successful.

Communication and Follow-up with Potential Clients: A Comprehensive Guide

1. Role

Communication and follow-up with potential customers play an important role in direct selling. This process is a vital step toward attracting potential customers to your product or service and converting them into a buyer. By communicating and following up properly, you can build stronger relationships with your potential customers and increase sales.

In this article, we will discuss strategies for effective communication and follow-up with prospects, including communication techniques, the importance of follow-up, and best practices.

2. Importance of communication

Effective communication with potential customers is not limited to just giving information; It is a process that helps build trust, identify needs, and solve problems.

2.1 Trust building

Through communication you can establish a trusting relationship with potential customers. When you present your offering clearly and honestly, customers develop trust in you.

2.2 Identification of needs

During communication, you can understand the needs and problems of potential customers. This information helps you make your product or service more relevant to them.

2.3 Solution of problems

When you solve potential customers' questions and problems, you can motivate them to adopt your product or service.

3. Strategies for effective communication

There are various strategies for effective communication with potential customers, which you can adopt to make your communication more effective.

3.1 Take a personal approach

Every potential customer is different, and their needs and preferences may also be different. Therefore, it is necessary to adopt a personal approach while communicating.

Tips:

- **Use customer information:** Use information about the customer's name, their company, and their professional interests.
- **Customized Message:** Tailor messages based on the customer's specific needs and problems.

3.2 Clear and concise messages

During communication, it is important to make the message clear and concise. Long and complex messages can confuse customers and lose their interest.

Tips:

- **Key points to note:** Include only the essential and key points in your message.
- **Use direct language:** Avoid complex words and technical jargon; Use simple and direct language.

3.3 Active listening

Active listening is essential during communication so you can understand the customer's needs and concerns.

Tips:

- **Ask questions:** Ask the customer open questions so you can understand their problems and needs.
- **Pay attention to feedback:** Listen carefully to customer reactions and feedback and respond to them appropriately.

3.4 Timely response

It is important to respond to potential customers' questions and inquiries in a timely manner. Responding quickly and effectively can strengthen your business's professional image.

Tips:

- **Reply immediately:** Respond as quickly as possible to keep the customer's attention.
- **Set response time:** Make sure you set a time for your answers and stick to it.

4. Importance of follow-up

The process of follow-up plays an important role in continuing communication with potential customers and keeping them interested in your product or service.

4.1 Relationship Building

Through follow-up you can establish a long-term relationship with the customer. This makes the customer feel that you care about their preferences and concerns.

4.2 Identification of opportunities

During follow-up, you can identify new opportunities for customers and their changing needs. This allows you to customize your offer.

4.3 Building trust and loyalty

Regular follow-up allows you to build trust and loyalty with the customer. When a customer sees that you care about them and give them good advice, they become more loyal to you.

5. Effective Follow-up Strategies

The following strategies can be adopted to make follow-up effective:

5.1 Follow-up at the right time

It is important to choose the right time for follow-up. Following up too early or too late may cause the customer to lose attention.

Tips:

- **time offset:** Schedule a follow-up based on the customer's preferences and their inquiries.
- **Time interval:** After the first follow-up, follow-up at regular intervals.

5.2 Use of different channels

Use different communication channels to follow-up so you can contact the customer through different means.

Tips:

- **Email:** Follow-up via email, including information and special offers about your product or service.
- **phone call:** Make phone calls for personal touch and quick resolution of customer queries.
- **Social Media:** Also follow up on social media and answer customer questions.

5.3 Provide value

During follow-up, provide valuable information and offers to the customer. This motivates them to show more interest in your offering.

Tips:

- **Special offer:** Provide special discounts or offers that encourage the customer to purchase your product.
- **Useful information:** Share useful industry related information and tips that can be beneficial to the customer.

5.4 Personal Contact

Maintain personal contact and address the client's specific needs during follow-up.

Tips:

- **Address by name:** Speak to the customer by name so they feel like you are communicating with them personally.
- **Relevant information:** Refer to the customer's previous conversations and their questions.

6. Tools and Technology for Follow-up

Various tools and techniques help make follow-up more effective and systematic.

6.1 CRM Software

CRM (Customer Relationship Management) software helps track potential customers' data and manage the process of follow-up.

Example:

- **Salesforce:** A leading CRM tool for lead tracking and follow-up.
- **HubSpot:** An all-in-one CRM and marketing automation platform.

6.2 Email Automation

Email automation tools help automatically send and track follow-up emails.

Example:

- **Mailchimp:** A popular software for creating and tracking email campaigns.
- **ActiveCampaign:** A platform for email automation and follow-up.

6.3 Task Management Tools

Task management tools help track and organize follow-up tasks.

Example:

- **Trello:** A tool for task management and tracking.
- **Asana:** A platform to manage team tasks and follow-up activities.

7. Analyzing and improving results

It is important to analyze the results of follow-up strategies and improve them so that you can make your processes more effective.

Tips:

- **Analyze it:** Analyze the results of follow-up activities and understand which methods are most effective.
- **Get Feedback:** Get feedback from customers and make improvements based on that.

conclusion

Communication and follow-up with potential customers are extremely important in direct selling. With effective communication and regular follow-up, you can build stronger relationships with potential customers, understand their needs, and increase sales. By using the right strategies, tools, and techniques, you can make your communications and follow-up more effective and increase the success of your business.

conclusion

Lead generation and prospecting are important aspects of network marketing. By using the right techniques and strategies, you can grow your business faster and attract more potential customers. In this chapter we discussed in detail various methods of lead generation, effective prospecting techniques, and strategies for converting leads into customers. In the next chapter, we will discuss important techniques of team building and leadership.

Chapter 06

Team Building and Leadership Skills

Chapter Introduction

Having a strong and dedicated team is extremely important to achieve success in network marketing. Team building and leadership techniques not only increase your team's productivity but also keep them motivated and dedicated. In this chapter, we will discuss the importance of effective team building, important leadership techniques, and motivation and communication.

art of team building

Team building is an important aspect in network marketing business, which determines the success of your business. By having a strong and dedicated team, you can promote your products and services more effectively, and build a larger customer base. In this article, we will discuss in detail various aspects of successful team building in network marketing.

importance of team building

1. **Business Growth:** With a strong team, your business's growth potential increases as your team members can also connect new customers and distributors.
2. **Training and Development:** A good team gives you and your members the opportunity to learn new skills and learn from each other.
3. **Support and Inspiration:** A good team provides an environment of collaboration and support, which helps all members stay motivated.

4. **Fixed Income:** With an expanded team, you can get stable income from different sources, because you don't rely only on your sales.

Team Building Strategies

recruiting the right people

Recruiting the right people in network marketing is an important process that plays a decisive role in the success of your business. The right people are those who are not only interested in your products and services but also have confidence in them and show seriousness about the business. Following are some effective strategies for identifying and recruiting the right people:

1. Identifying the target market

The first step to recruiting the right people is to identify your target market.

- **Personal Characteristics:** Target people who have characteristics like leadership skills, a positive attitude, and a willingness to learn.
- **Age and Occupation:** Keeping in mind the demand for your products, analyze the age group and professional background.

2. Attraction Marketing

Attraction marketing means presenting yourself in such a way that qualified and interested people are attracted to you.

- **Personal Branding:** Build a strong personal brand that reflects your business ethics and values.
- **online presence:** Be active on social media and online platforms, and share your success stories.

3. Use referral programs

This can be an effective way to add new members through current team members.

- **Incentive:** Give current members incentives for recommending new people, such as bonuses or special rewards.
- **Focus on quality:** Set some criteria to ensure the quality of referrals.

4. Interview Process

Develop an interview process that helps you assess the suitability of potential members.

- **Interview Questions:** Prepare questions that reveal their vision, purpose, and dedication to their business.
- **Personal Conversation:** Have personal conversations with potential members so you can better understand their interests and objectives.

5. Trial period

Establish a trial period so you can assess new members' performance and their commitment to the business.

- **Initial Projects:** Give them a chance to work on some initial projects so you can understand their capabilities.
- **Feedback and Guidance:** Give them feedback regularly and provide guidance as needed.

6. Evaluation and Optimization

Regular evaluation and optimization of the recruitment process is essential so that you can improve your recruitment strategies.

- **Review and Analysis:** Review the recruitment process regularly and see which areas need improvement.
- **problem solution:** If there are problems in recruitment, make plans to solve them.

training and development

Training and development is a vital process in network marketing, providing your team members with the skills and knowledge they need to succeed in business. A well-trained team contributes to the growth of your business and ensures stability and success in the long term. Here are some strategies through which you can make your team's training and development effective:

1. Initial Training Program

initial training program There is a required step for new members, in which they are taught the basics of the business.

- **product knowledge:** Provide in-depth information about your products and services so they can speak to customers with confidence.
- **Business Model:** Explain the business model of network marketing, including commission structure and team building strategies.

2. Regular training sessions

Regular training sessions help keep your members updated with the latest information and strategies.

- **Weekly Webinars and Seminars:** Invite experts who can motivate team members and keep them up to date on the latest marketing trends.
- **Online Learning Platform:** Use various online platforms where members can learn at their own pace and develop new skills.

3. Skill Development

Focusing on skills development helps members in their personal and professional development.

- **Leadership Skills:** Organize specialized workshops to develop leadership skills so that members can effectively lead their teams.
- **Communication Skills:** Provide training on effective communication skills so members can better communicate with their customers and team.

4. Mentorship Program

An effective mentorship program provides guidance and support to members.

- **Experienced Mentors:** Appoint experienced members as mentors for new members so that they can learn from their experience.
- **Personal Advice:** Mentors meet with members regularly to review their progress, as well as provide them with personal advice.

5. Evaluation of progress

Regular evaluation of progress is necessary so that the efficiency and performance of the members can be assessed.

- **Evaluation metrics:** Establish some metrics to assess members' progress, such as sales figures, team expansion, and customer satisfaction.
- **Feedback System:** Take feedback from members and give them feedback on their performance so that they can improve their weak areas.

6. Motivation and encouragement

Motivating and encouraging members is important to increase their productivity and dedication.

- **Rewards and Incentives:** Provide rewards and incentives to members for good performance, such as bonuses, trips, or special recognition.

- **Success Stories:** Share success stories of team members so that other members are inspired and realize what is possible in business.

7. Continuous learning environment

Create an environment that encourages continuous learning and growth.

- **Knowledge Sharing:** Encourage team members to share their experiences and knowledge with each other.
- **Collaboration and Support:** Create a collaborative and supportive environment where members are always ready to help each other.

Effective communication with the team

In network marketing, effective communication with the team is extremely important for the success of your team and business growth. Communication not only exchanges information but also helps in keeping team members united, solving problems and increasing their productivity. Here are some effective ways through which you can communicate with your team:

1. Regular meetings

Regular meetings are a great way to connect with your team members and discuss important issues.

- **Weekly Team Meetings:** Hold a team meeting at a set time each week so you can review everyone's progress and make plans for the next week.

- **Set the agenda:** Each meeting should have a clear agenda so that the conversation remains focused and all essential topics can be discussed.

2. Use of digital communication tools

Digital communication tools are an effective means of staying connected with your team, especially when your team members are in different locations.

- **Messaging Apps:** Use apps like WhatsApp, Slack, or Telegram to send and receive messages instantly.
- **Video Conferencing:** Do video conferencing using Zoom, Google Meet, or Microsoft Teams, so you can have face-to-face conversations.

3. Open Communication Culture

Create an environment where all members can openly share their opinions and ideas.

- **Quiz Session:** Organize regular question-and-answer sessions where members can ask questions and give suggestions on any issue.
- **Welcome Feedback:** Encourage all members to provide feedback and take their concerns seriously.

4. Team Newsletter

You can share information regularly through a team newsletter.

- **Monthly Newsletter:** Release a monthly newsletter that highlights team successes, upcoming events, and important announcements.
- **Participation of members:** Motivate subscribers to contribute content to the newsletter, making them feel included.

5. Inspiration and support

Keeping members motivated and supported increases their productivity and their commitment to the team.

- **Praise and Recognition:** Publicly praise and honor members for their good work.
- **Incentive Program:** Organize special events or activities to encourage members' efforts.

6. Communicate to solve problems

Any problem within the team can be solved only through communication.

- **Identification of problems:** Sit down with the team regularly to identify potential problems and find solutions.
- **Shared Decision:** Involve team members in the decision process so that they feel more responsible for the decisions.

7. Team Building Activities

Team building activities promote communication and strengthen relationships among members.

- **Outdoor Activities:** Organize activities like picnics, trekking, or team lunches that allow members to connect with each other in an informal way.
- **Workshops and Games:** Organize workshops and games that help team members understand each other better.

setting goals and objectives

Establishing goals and objectives in network marketing is essential to guide your team in the right direction. Without clear and achievable goals, team members may have difficulty understanding what efforts to focus on. Goals not only provide direction, but also motivation and a sense of accomplishment. Here are some steps through which you can set effective goals and objectives for your team:

1. Clear and achievable goals

Goals should be clear and achievable so that members can maintain their commitment to them.

- **Specificity:** Goals should be specific. For example, "Add 10 new customers by the end of the month" is a typical goal.
- **Measurability:** Goals should be measurable so you can monitor progress. For example, a sales goal is a measurable goal.

- **Achievability:** Goals should be realistic and achievable so that members do not become discouraged.
- **Relevance:** Goals should be consistent with the overall objectives of the business.
- **Time-bound:** There should be a specific time limit for the goal. For example, "20% sales growth within three months" is a time-bound goal.

2. Short and long term goals

A combination of short and long term goals keeps members motivated for the immediate and the future.

- **Short Term Goals:** These can be achieved quickly and pave the way for progress towards long-term goals. For example, "To recruit two new members by next week."
- **long term goals:** These take time and require a comprehensive approach. For example, "Doubling the team size within a year."

3. Team involvement

As the participation of team members increases in the process of setting goals, their responsibility and commitment also increases.

- **Brainstorming Session:** Hold brainstorming sessions with the team so that all members can share their ideas and suggestions.
- **Participation:** Involve members in the goal setting process so they feel more responsible for it.

4. Progress monitoring

Regular monitoring of progress is essential so you can ensure that your team is moving in the right direction.

- **Progress Report:** Prepare progress reports regularly and share with the team.
- **Evaluation metrics:** Set some evaluation metrics for goal achievement, such as sales numbers, new hires, etc.

5. Feedback and Improvement

Taking feedback and making improvements based on it can increase the efficiency of your team.

- **Feedback from members:** Get regular feedback from members so you can understand their concerns and suggestions.
- **Timely Correction:** Modify goals and plans as needed so they remain practical and achievable.

6. Motivation and encouragement

It is very important to motivate and encourage the members to achieve the goal.

- **Awards and recognition:** Provide rewards and recognition to members who achieve goals.
- **Celebration:** Celebrate goal achievement and share success stories.

7. Timely re-evaluation

It is important to re-evaluate goals and objectives from time to time to ensure that they are consistent with changing business conditions.

- **Annual Review:** Review all goals and objectives at least once a year and update them as needed.
- **problem solution:** If there are any problems in achieving the goals, identify them and make a plan to solve them.

inspiration and recognition

Motivation and recognition in network marketing is essential to keep your team members excited and dedicated to their work. Motivated members are not only more productive, but they also encourage other members of their team. Receiving recognition makes members realize the importance of their work and motivate them to further improve their efforts. Here are some ways through which you can motivate and recognize your team members:

1. Personal recognition

Personal recognition An effective way to make members feel special.

- **Appreciation Letter:** Send appreciation letters to members for their excellent performance, making special mention of their contributions.
- **Personal Message:** Praise them in person or via text message and thank them for their efforts.

2. Public recognition

publicly recognized Achieving makes members feel proud and confident.

- **Appreciation in team meeting:** Publicly recognize members' accomplishments during team meetings and appreciate their efforts.
- **Mentioned in Newsletter:** Mention outstanding performing members and share their accomplishments in the team newsletter.

3. Sharing inspirational stories

Inspirational stories encourage members to achieve their goals.

- **Success Stories:** Share success stories in team meetings and invite members who have excelled to talk about their journey and strategies.
- **Inspirational Video:** Share inspirational videos that offer positive attitudes and success stories to motivate members.

4. Rewards and Incentive Programs

Rewards and incentive programs provide additional motivation for members to achieve their goals.

- **Bonuses and Rewards:** Offer bonuses or special rewards to high-performing members, such as cash awards, gift cards, or special gifts.
- **competition:** Encourage healthy competition within the team and recognize the winners.

5. Opportunities for personal development

Provide members with personal development opportunities so they can hone their skills and advance in their careers.

- **Training Programme:** Organize specialized training and workshops for members to help enhance their skills and knowledge.
- **Career Development Plans:** Create career development plans for members so they clearly understand their career goals and are motivated to achieve them.

6. Collaborative environment

Create a collaborative environment where all members can contribute to each other's success.

- **Team Building Activities:** Organize team building activities to strengthen relationships among team members.
- **Shared Goals:** Motivate all members to work towards a common goal, thereby increasing their unity and dedication.

7. Timely Feedback

Provide timely feedback to members so that they can remain aware of their actions and make necessary improvements.

- **Regular Reviews:** Regularly conduct performance reviews of members and give them honest feedback about their performance.

- **Constructive response:** Provide positive and constructive feedback so that members can identify their weak areas and improve them.

qualities of effective leadership

Effective leadership is important in network marketing, as a strong leader motivates his team, guides them in the right direction, and contributes significantly to the success of the business. The qualities and abilities required for effective leadership are wide-ranging, and these qualities make a leader not only effective but also keep their team members motivated and dedicated.

1. Perspective and clarity

Approach And **clarity** These are the hallmarks of an effective leader. A leader needs a clear vision and goals so that they can guide their team in the right direction.

- **Future Vision:** An effective leader must have a clear understanding of future goals and plans. They must be able to clearly see and communicate the direction of growth of their business.
- **Clarity of goals:** The leader must present clear and achievable goals to the team. This clarity motivates team members to work in the right direction.

2. Inspirational potential

inspirational ability One of the most important qualities of a leader. A good leader inspires his team, encourages them, and appreciates their efforts.

- **Enthusiasm and Energy:** The enthusiasm and energy of the leader positively influences the team and motivates them to achieve their goals.
- **Success Stories:** Sharing your experiences and success stories motivates team members and makes them believe that success is possible.

3. Communication Skills

communication skills are essential for effective leadership. A good leader can share his or her views and listen to others in a clear and effective manner.

- **Hearing Ability:** Effective leaders are good listeners. They listen to and respect the concerns and ideas of their team members.
- **Clarity and Accuracy:** While communicating, the leader must be clear and precise so that there is no misunderstanding.

4. Decision making ability

decision making ability A leader has power. An effective leader must have the ability to take accurate and quick decisions, which are beneficial to the team and the business.

- **Analysis and Assessment:** A good leader analyzes various options and selects the most effective option.

- **Implementation of the decision**: After taking a decision, the leader must have the ability to implement it effectively.

5. Problem Solving Skills

problem solving skills Helps an effective leader solve problems that may affect team performance.

- **Problem Identification**: A leader must identify problems quickly and make plans to solve them.
- **Creative Solutions**: The leader must have the ability to present creative and practical solutions.

6. Team Building

team building is important for an effective leader. A leader must have the ability to keep his team united and dedicated.

- **Trust and Cooperation**: A good leader fosters trust and cooperation among his team members.
- **Utilization of team strengths**: The leader utilizes and aggregates the strengths and abilities of each team member.

7. Self-motivation and discipline

self-motivation and discipline Keeps a leader motivated and organized personally and professionally.

- **Self-Motivation:** An effective leader must be self-motivated towards his goals and disciplined in his actions.
- **Discipline:** By following discipline the leader can achieve his own goals and can also keep his team disciplined.

8. Empathy and understanding

empathy and understanding Helps a leader build stronger relationships with his team members.

- **Sympathy:** A good leader understands the feelings and problems of his team members and provides support to them.
- **Understanding and Support:** The leader must understand and support the personal and professional needs of team members.

9. Ability to adapt to change

ability to adapt to change Helps an effective leader to adapt to changing circumstances with time.

- **Flexible Approach:** A good leader has the ability to change and adapt his strategies according to circumstances.
- **Novelty welcome:** The leader should be able to adopt new technologies and methods and inspire his team to adopt the same.

10. Ethics and honesty

ethics and honesty The most important qualities of an effective leader are. A leader must be moral and honest so that he can become a role model for his members.

- **Honesty:** A good leader acts with integrity and maintains transparency in his actions and decisions.
- **ethics:** Adhering to ethical values helps a leader maintain the respect and trust of his team.

Strategies to motivate and retain the team

To motivate and retain the team, it is first essential that you set clear and achievable goals and objectives.

- **Clarity of goals:** Without clear goals and objectives, the team may lack direction and purpose. Make sure all members know where they are headed and what their goals are.
- **Compatible Purpose:** Make sure the team's goals align with individual goals and the overall objectives of the business. This inspires everyone to work in the same direction.

2. Regular communication and feedback

Regular communication and feedback with the team plays an important role in maintaining motivation.

- **Regular Meetings:** Hold weekly or monthly meetings where team members can review their progress and discuss upcoming challenges.

- **Feedback and Discussion:** Provide regular feedback to team members and take their problems and suggestions seriously. This communication motivates them for better performance and increases their self-confidence.

3. Incentives and Rewards

Incentives and rewards are an effective way to recognize team members for their efforts and successes.

- **Inspirational Awards:** Give rewards and recognition to members who perform outstandingly. These prizes can be cash prizes, gift cards, or special gifts.
- **Celebrations and Honors:** Celebrate team successes and publicly honor members. This motivates them more and makes their efforts appreciated.

4. Training and development opportunities

Providing members with opportunities for personal and professional development helps maintain their motivation.

- **Training Programme:** Organize regular training and workshops that help members learn new skills and improve existing skills.
- **Personal Development:** Guide the member towards personal development and provide them with opportunities that inspire their professional growth.

5. Create a supportive environment

A supportive and collaborative environment is important to keep team members motivated and engaged.

- **Team Building Activities:** Organize team building activities that foster trust and collaboration among team members. These activities may include group sports, outdoor events, and social gatherings.
- **support system:** Establish a strong support system in which team members can seek solutions to their problems and get the help they need.

6. Personal attention and recognition

Personal attention and recognition make team members feel special and maintain their motivation.

- **Personal communication:** Interact personally from time to time and appreciate the efforts and achievements of members.
- **Freedom and Responsibility:** Give responsibility to members and recognize their decisions. This makes them self-reliant and motivated.

7. Positive attitude and mindset

A positive attitude and mindset plays an important role in maintaining the motivation of team members.

- **Enthusiasm and inspiration:** Maintain enthusiasm and positivity in your behavior, which motivates team members.
- **Positive results:** Share positive results and success stories that motivate team members and get them excited to achieve their goals.

8. Embrace change and innovation

Change and innovation motivates team members and motivates them to stay engaged in the business.

- **New Strategies:** Adopt new marketing strategies and techniques and inspire the team to use them.
- **Novelty:** Organize new and interesting activities and incentives that provide team members with new energy and motivation in the business.

9. Conflict Resolution and Problem Management

Resolving conflicts and problems effectively helps maintain the motivation of team members.

- **problem solution:** Quickly and effectively resolve problems and conflicts that arise within the team.
- **Empathy and understanding:** Demonstrate empathy and understanding when resolving problems and make team members feel that their concerns are being taken seriously.

10. Support health and well-being

Paying attention to the well-being and health of members helps maintain their motivation and productivity.

- **Health Programme:** Provide health and wellness programs for team members, such as fitness workshops or mental health seminars.
- **Work-Life Balance:** Provide flexible working hours and facilities to maintain work-life balance.

Motivating and retaining a team in network marketing is an ongoing process that can be done through effective leadership, motivation, support, and development. Clear goals and objectives, regular communication and feedback, incentives and rewards, training and development opportunities, supportive environment, individual attention and recognition, positive attitudes, innovation, conflict resolution, and health and well-being support—all these elements motivate and Are important for long term retention. By implementing these strategies, you can keep your team motivated and dedicated, which will contribute significantly to the success and growth of the business.

conclusion

Team building and leadership are important elements to achieving success in network marketing. By building a strong and dedicated team and using effective leadership techniques, you can increase your team's productivity and make them motivated and dedicated. In this chapter we discussed in detail the importance of effective team building, important leadership techniques, and motivation and communication. In the next chapter, we will discuss strategies for building long-term relationships with customers in network marketing.

Chapter 07

Analyzing and improving results

Chapter Introduction

Analyzing and improving results in network marketing is an important process that helps you understand and improve the effectiveness of your marketing campaigns. Here the process is explained in detail:

<u>Analysis of Results</u>

1.Data Collection

Gathering data from various sources such as website analytics, social media analytics, email campaign data, and sales reports.

2.Key Performance Indicators (KPIs)

Selecting KPIs that are important to your business. Such as: number of leads, conversion rate, customer acquisition cost (CAC), customer lifetime value (CLV).

3.Data Analysis

Analyzing data using various analytical tools and software.

Analyzing customer behavior, sales patterns, and the effectiveness of marketing campaigns.

4.Review of Performance Metrics

Identifying areas where performance has been good and improving those areas **Identifying where improvement is needed.**

<u>Improvement</u>

1.Strategy Adjustment

Adjusting marketing strategies that are not producing expected results.

Creating new strategies and plans that can be more effective.

2.A/B Testing

A/B testing different strategies and campaigns to understand which strategy is most effective.

Making changes to marketing campaigns based on test results.

3.Customer Feedback

Taking direct feedback from customers.

To improve the product or service based on their experiences and suggestions.

4.Use of AI and Machine Learning

Using AI based tools that can analyze large data sets and provide insights for improvement.

Using machine learning models to predict which strategies will be most effective.

Continuous Monitoring

Continuously monitoring marketing campaigns and reviewing them regularly.

Analyzing data in real time and taking quick decisions.

Team Training

Providing training to the team on latest analytical tools and techniques.

Keeping the team aware of new marketing trends and best practices.

Conclusion

Analyzing and improving results in network marketing is a continuous process. This ensures that your marketing efforts continue to become more efficient and effective over time. Through regular analysis and strategy adjustment, you can maintain your business growth and attract more customers.

Chapter

08

Use of digital tools and techniques in network marketing

Chapter Introduction

In the digital age, the use of digital tools and techniques has become essential to conduct network marketing effectively. Correct use of these tools and techniques not only expands your reach but also automates and simplifies your tasks. In this chapter, we will discuss various digital tools and techniques that can be helpful in growing your business in network marketing.

social media platform

Social media platforms have brought a revolutionary change in the field of network marketing. These platforms have proven to be a boon for network marketing professionals as they help in massively expanding the reach of the business, attracting new customers, and organizing and motivating the team. In this article, we will see how social media platforms can prove to be a boon in network marketing and how they can be used effectively.

1. Wider reach and exposure

social media Platforms provide businesses with global reach. For network marketing, this can be a great source of opportunity and profit.

- **Global Audience:** Through social media, network marketing businesses can market their services and products to a global audience. This expands the reach of the business beyond limited geographical boundaries and increases the circle of potential customers.

- **Viral Promotion:** A well-designed post or campaign on social media can quickly go viral, increasing business recognition and product popularity.

2. Targeted Marketing and Advertising

Through targeted marketing and advertising on social media platforms, network marketing businesses can effectively reach their target customers.

- **Demographic Targeting:** Social media platforms like Facebook and Instagram allow you to target ads based on various demographic and geographic criteria. This ensures that your ad reaches the right audience.
- **Public Posts and Advertisements:** Through paid advertising, you can showcase your product or service to a specific target audience, increasing your sales and brand recognition.

3. Brand building and management

Social media platforms are an important tool of brand building and management for network marketing businesses.

- **brand recognition:** A consistent and engaging social media profile strengthens your brand identity. It helps in building and maintaining the image of your business.
- **Brand Message:** Through social media, you can share your brand's message and beliefs directly with your audience, increasing your brand's credibility and identity.

4. Interaction and support with customers

Social media platforms allow network marketing businesses to communicate directly with customers.

- **Direct communication:** On social media, you can quickly answer customers' questions and address their concerns. This improves customer service and increases customer satisfaction.
- **Feedbacks and Suggestions:** Through feedback and suggestions received from customers, you can improve your products and services and maintain the quality of your business.

5. Collaboration and motivation with the team

Social media platforms are also useful for promoting collaboration and motivation within the team.

- **Team Groups:** Groups can be created for teams on various social media platforms such as Facebook and WhatsApp, where team members can share their information, ideas, and inspiration.
- **Inspirational Content:** By regularly sharing inspirational and informative content, you can inspire your team and motivate them to move toward their goals.

6. Content Marketing and Education

Through content marketing on social media, network marketing businesses can educate and inform their audiences.

- **Blogs and Articles:** You can share your business blogs or articles on social media, providing your audience with useful information and advice.
- **Video Tutorials:** By hosting video tutorials and live sessions, you can teach your audience about products and services and solve their problems.

7. Tracking and Analysis

Social media platforms also allow you to measure and analyze the success of your marketing campaigns.

- **Analytics Tools:** Through the analytics tools available on social media platforms, you can measure the effectiveness of your campaigns, such as post reach, engagement rates, and ad performance.

- **Data Driven Decision:** Based on analytics, you can take data driven decisions and improve your marketing campaigns, making your strategies more effective.

equipment

1.Facebook: Create your business's page on Facebook, post regularly, and run ads. Join related groups and promote your products using Facebook Groups.

2.Instagram: Post attractive photos and videos on Instagram. Use Instagram Stories and Reels. Use effective hashtags.

3.LinkedIn: Expand your professional network on LinkedIn. Share your experiences and knowledge through LinkedIn articles and posts.

4.Twitter: Tweet regularly on Twitter. Use trending hashtags and participate in related conversations.

5.Youtube: Create and upload videos about your products and services on YouTube. Share video tutorials, webinars, and customer testimonials.

email marketing tools

Email marketing tools help you maintain regular communication with your customers and prospects.

1.MailChimp: Create and send engaging email campaigns using MailChimp. Observe email performance through its analytical tools.

2.Constant Contact: Create professional email templates and use automation features using Constant Contact.

3.SendinBlue: SendinBlue Run email and SMS marketing campaigns through. This tool also lets you set up automated workflows.

4.GetResponse: Host webinars and manage email marketing campaigns using GetResponse. Also use its landing page builder.

Customer Relationship Management (CRM) Tools

CRM tools simplify relationship management with your customers and streamline your business operations.

1. Salesforce: Salesforce is a comprehensive CRM solution that helps you manage your customer data and automate your sales processes.

2.HubSpot: Using HubSpot you can track all interactions with your customers and optimize your sales and marketing strategies.

3.Zoho CRM: Zoho CRM provides customizable solutions for your business and helps manage relationships with your customers.

4.Pipedrive: Pipedrive is a sales pipeline management tool that streamlines your sales process and keeps your team focused.

Automation and Productivity Tools

Automation and productivity tools save your time and automate your tasks.

1.Zapier: Using Zapier you can connect different applications together and automate your tasks.

2.IFTTT: Using IFTTT you can create automated workflows between different digital services.

3.Trello: Trello Manage your projects and tasks using. Organize your tasks using its board and card system.

4.Asana: Collaborate with your team and track your projects using Asana.

Data Analytics and Tracking Tools

Data analytics and tracking tools help you measure your performance and optimize your strategies.

1.Google Analytics: Analyze your website traffic and user behavior using Google Analytics.

2.Hotjar: View heatmaps and recordings of your website users using Hotjar.

3.SEMrush: Analyze your SEO performance using SEMrush and check your competition.

4.Table: Visualize your data using Tableau and gain important insights.

conclusion

Digital tools and techniques play an important role in growing your business rapidly in network marketing. By making proper use of social media platforms, email marketing, CRM, automation and productivity, and data analytics tools, you can easily achieve your goals and build stronger relationships with your customers. In this chapter, we discussed various digital tools and technologies in detail. In the next chapter, we will discuss the challenges and their solutions in network marketing.

Chapter
09

Challenges and their solutions in network marketing

Chapter Introduction

Achieving success in network marketing can be challenging. There are many types of obstacles and challenges to be faced in this sector, but with the right strategies and approach these challenges can be overcome. In this chapter, we will discuss in detail the commonly encountered challenges in network marketing and their solutions.

Commonly Encountered Challenges

1. Finding and hiring the right people

challenge

Getting the right and qualified people to join your team can be a major challenge. Many times, new members are skeptical about network marketing or lack adequate motivation and support.

Solution

- **Targeted Recruitment:** Identify your target audience and tailor your recruitment strategy to their needs and desires.

- **Clear information:** Provide potential members with clear and accurate information about network marketing. Explain to them the benefits and prospects of the business.

-**Training and Support:** Provide proper training and support to new members so they feel confident and competent in the business.

2. Maintain constant motivation and dedication

challenge

It is important to maintain constant motivation and dedication to achieve success in network marketing. But sometimes the enthusiasm of members may wane over time.

Solution

-Goal Setting: Set clear and realistic goals with team members and motivate them regularly.

-Awards and recognition: Recognize and reward members' achievements. This will increase their motivation and dedication.

-Regular communication: Maintain regular communication with team members and listen and address their concerns and problems.

3. Maintaining product and service quality

challenge

Providing high quality products and services is essential to network marketing success. Maintaining customer satisfaction and loyalty can be challenging.

Solution

-Quality Control: Regularly inspect the quality of products and services and ensure they meet high standards.

-Customer Feedback: Collect feedback from customers regularly and make improvements based on their suggestions and concerns.

-**Trained Staff:** Train your team to provide high quality products and services.

4. Facing competition

challenge

Facing competition in network marketing can be a big challenge. There are many companies and products available in the market, which can make it difficult to attract potential customers for your business.

Solution

-**Different identity:** Highlight the uniqueness and features of your product or service. Make your business different from competitors.

-**Relationship Building:** Build strong and long-term relationships with customers. Understand their needs and desires and provide them personalized services.

-**innovation:** Develop innovative products and services and adapt your business to changing market requirements.

5. Time Management

challenge

Proper management of time is important to achieve success in network marketing. At times, it can be difficult to strike a balance between various tasks and responsibilities.

Solution

-Priority Setting: Prioritize your tasks and focus on the most important ones.

-Task division: Divide tasks and share responsibilities with team members.

-Tools and Techniques: Use digital tools and technologies for time management, such as task management apps and calendars.

6. Financial Management

challenge

Financial management is an important aspect, especially when you are growing your network marketing business. Lack of correct financial strategies can cause problems in business.

Solution

-Budget Determination: Prepare a clear and realistic budget and

Control your expenses.

-financial records: Regularly update financial records and analyze financial performance.

-Financial Consulting: If necessary, consult a financial advisor and tweak your financial plans.

<u>Learning from Failure</u>

Failure is an inevitable part of life. It is the process through which we gain experience, learn, and grow. Failure gives a direction to our life and teaches us how to achieve our goals. In this chapter, we will discuss in detail the importance of failure, its various aspects, and ways to learn from failure.

1. Importance of failure

The importance of failure can be seen in several forms:

1.Source of Experience: Failure helps us gain experience. It gives us an opportunity to identify mistakes which we can correct in the future.

2. Source of Inspiration: Failure motivates us. It helps us understand what we are doing wrong and motivates us to work harder to achieve our goals.

3.Development of tolerance: Through failure we develop tolerance. It teaches us patience and perseverance, which are important in every aspect of our life.

4.Source of Innovation: Failure inspires us to adopt new ideas and approaches. It helps us discover ways that can help us achieve our goals.

5.Improving social relations: Failure improves our social relationships. It teaches us how to behave with others with empathy and understanding.

2. Different types of failure

There are many types of failure, some of the major ones are:

1. Personal failure: This is the failure that happens in our personal life. It is linked to our personal goals, relationships, and self-esteem.

2.Business Failure: This is the failure that happens in our business life. It is related to our career, business, and professional goals.

3.Academic failure: This is the failure that happens in our educational life. It is related to our studies, examinations, and educational goals.

4.Social Failure: This is the failure that occurs in our social life. It is related to our social relationships, friendships, and social goals.

3. Ways to learn from failure

There are many ways to learn from failure, some of the major ones are:

1. Self-Analysis: The first step to learning from failure is self-analysis. We have to understand where we went wrong and what we did wrong. It helps us to recognize our mistakes and correct them.

2.Positive Attitude: A positive attitude is important to learn from failure. We should see failure as an opportunity, not an obstacle.

3.Resetting goals To learn from failure, we must reset our goals. Make sure that our goals are according to SMART (Specific, Measurable, Achievable, Relevant, Time-bound) criteria.

4.Getting Support: It is important to have support to learn from failure. This support can come from our family, friends, and coworkers.

5.Patience and perseverance: Learning from failure requires patience and perseverance. We have to understand that failure is a process and it will take time for us to recover from it.

4. Examples of failure and learning from them

There are many inspiring examples of failure from which we can learn a lot:

1.Thomas Edison: The life of Thomas Edison is an excellent example of learning from failure. He invented the bulb after failing more than 1,000 times. He said, "I didn't fail, I found 1,000 ways that don't work."

2.Mahatma Gandhi: The life of Mahatma Gandhi is also an inspiring example of learning from failure. He faced failure many times, but he never gave up his goal and ultimately led India to independence.

3.Abraham Lincoln: The life of Abraham Lincoln is also an inspiring example of learning from failure. He faced defeat in the elections several times, but he never gave up his goal and eventually became the President of America.

4.Steve Jobs: The life of Steve Jobs is also an inspiring example of learning from failure. He was fired from his own company Apple, but he did not give up and came back and made Apple one of the most successful companies in the world.

5.JK Rowling: J.K. Rowling's life is also an inspiring example of learning from failure. He faced many failures, but he did not give up and eventually wrote the Harry Potter series, which made him world famous.

5. Practical solutions to recover from failure

There are many practical measures to recover from failure, some of the major ones are:

1.Self-sensation: We should be sensitive towards ourselves. Instead of blaming ourselves after failure, we should motivate ourselves and be ready to move forward.

2.Taking Small Steps: We should overcome failure by taking small steps. It motivates us to achieve our goals and gives us confidence that we can do it.

3.Taking time: It is important to take time to recover from failure. We need time to learn from our mistakes and correct them.

4.Positive Thinking: Positive thinking helps us recover from failure. We must have confidence in our abilities and believe that we can achieve our goals.

5.Getting Help: We must get help to recover from failure. This support can come from our family, friends, and coworkers.

6.Health care: It is important to take care of physical and mental health. Regular exercise, healthy eating, and adequate sleep help us recover from failure.

6. Myths related to failure

There are many myths related to failure, some of the prominent ones are:

1.Failure means we are unworthy: This is a myth. Failure does not mean that we are worthless. It is simply a process by which we learn and grow.

2.Failure means we can never achieve our goals: This is also a myth. Failure does not mean that we cannot achieve our goals. It's just an obstacle we can overcome.

3.Failure means we should give up: This is also a myth. Failure does not mean that we should give up. This is just an opportunity from which we can learn and achieve our goals.

4.Failure means that we should not take help from others: This is also a myth. Failure does not mean that we should not take help from others. Seeking help is a sign that we are serious about achieving our goals.

5. Failure means we must blame ourselves: This is also a myth. Failure does not mean that we should blame ourselves. It is simply a process through which we can learn and grow.

conclusion

There are many challenges to be faced in network marketing, but with the right approach and strategies these challenges can be successfully overcome. In this chapter, we discussed in detail the commonly encountered challenges in network marketing and their solutions. In the next chapter, we will discuss the mindset and approach needed to achieve success in network marketing.

Chapter 10

Mindset and Approach Required for Success in Network Marketing

Introduction

Achieving success in network marketing requires the right mindset and approach. It is not limited to just selling products and recruiting people, but it requires a positive mindset, determination, and constant self-development. In this chapter, we will discuss in detail the mindset and approach required to achieve success in network marketing.

importance of positive mindset

A positive mindset is the key to success in network marketing. It helps you face challenges and move forward even in difficult times.

1.Self-confidence: Self-confidence is an important element of success. Have faith in yourself and believe that you can achieve your goals.

2.Positive Thinking: Positive thinking removes negativity and doubt. Keep your thinking positive and stay focused on your objectives.

3.Patience: Success in network marketing is a long journey. Be patient and keep trying.

self development and education

Self-development and continued education are vital to success in network marketing.

1.Regular Training: Attend training programs regularly to enhance your knowledge and skills.

2.Books and Articles: Read books and articles on network marketing, leadership, and personal development.

3.Webinars and Seminars: Attend webinars and seminars conducted by industry experts and successful network marketers.

goal setting and planning

The importance of goal setting and achievement is very important in the life of any person or organization. This is an important aspect of achieving success and it is essential to understand and implement it correctly. In this chapter, we will discuss in detail various aspects of goal setting and its achievement.

1. Importance of goal

Goal is a standard that determines the direction of our life. Without it, our efforts are without direction, and we experience imbalance and disorganization in our lives. Goals motivate us and encourage us to move forward towards achieving our dreams.

2. Principles of goal setting

Following are some important principles of goal setting:

2.1 SMART principle

According to SMART principle, goals should be Specific, Measurable, Achievable, Relevant and Time-bound.

- Specific: The goal should be clear and concise. This maintains clarity in the direction of achieving the goal.
- Measurable: Goals should be measurable so that we can track our progress.
- Achievable: The goal should be realistic and achievable.

- Relevant: Goals should be related to other important areas of our life.
- Time-bound: There should be a fixed time limit for the goal so that we can complete it on time.

2.2 Challenging but achievable goals

Goals should be challenging so that they motivate us to push our limits. However, one must ensure that they are achievable, to avoid disappointment and frustration.

2.3 Short and long term goals

Both short and long term goals should be kept in mind. Short-term goals give us quick results and maintain our motivation, while long-term goals guide us towards bigger goals in our life.

3. Goal setting process

The goal setting process can be divided into several stages:

3.1 Self-analysis

The first step in the goal setting process is self-analysis. In this we have to analyze various aspects of our life, such as our values, interests, skills and aspirations. This helps us understand what we really want and in which direction we should focus our efforts.

3.2 Setting priorities

After introspection, we have to determine our priorities. For this, we should maintain balance in various areas of our life, such as career, personal development, health, relationships etc. Setting priorities helps us understand which goals are most important to us.

3.3 Goal setting

After setting priorities, we have to set our goals. For this the SMART principle should be followed. We must make our goals clear, measurable, achievable, relatable and time bound.

3.4 Making action plan

After setting goals, we have to make an action plan. This plan tells us what steps we need to take to achieve our goals. The following points should be included in the action plan:

- Identification of required resources
- Major Steps and Milestones
- time limit
- Possible obstacles and their solutions

3.5 Implementation and Monitoring

After making an action plan, we have to implement it. This is the most important step, because without implementation, our goal remains just a dream. We should regularly monitor our progress and modify our plan as necessary.

4. Skills required to achieve goals

Some important skills are required to achieve the goal:

4.1 Time Management

Time management is an important skill which helps in achieving goals. We should use our time properly and divide our tasks on the basis of priority.

4.2 Staying organized

Staying organized also plays an important role in achieving goals. We should keep our workplace, work materials and time table organized.

4.3 Problem Solving

Problems may arise in the path of achieving the goal. Problem solving skills help us to identify these problems, analyze them and find solutions.

4.4 Self-motivation

Self-motivation helps us to continuously strive towards our goals. We should use various techniques to keep ourselves motivated, such as positive thinking, self-realization, and studying inspirational literature.

4.5 Continuous learning

Continuous learning is also important in achieving goals. We must learn regularly to develop our skills and acquire new knowledge.

5. Obstacles coming in the way of achieving the goal

Many obstacles may come in the way of achieving the goal. Some of these major obstacles are:

5.1 Self-doubt

Self-doubt weakens our self-confidence and hinders us from achieving our goals. We should resort to positive thinking and self-motivation to overcome self-doubt.

5.2 Fear of failure

Fear of failure can also become an obstacle in achieving our goals. We should understand that failure is a part of success and it gives us an opportunity to learn.

5.3 Lack of time

Lack of time can also become a hindrance in achieving the goal. We should manage our time properly and divide our tasks based on priorities.

5.4 External pressure

External pressure, such as pressure from family, society, and workplace, can also hinder us from achieving our goals. We must remain dedicated to our goals and manage external pressure properly.

5.5 Laziness

Laziness can also be a major obstacle in achieving goals. To overcome our laziness, we should exercise regularly, eat a healthy diet, and sleep at regular times.

6. Inspirational stories to achieve goals

To get inspiration to achieve our goals, we should take inspiration from the stories of great people. Here are some inspirational stories that can help us achieve our goals:

6.1 Abraham Lincoln

The story of Abraham Lincoln teaches us that despite failures, we should continue to strive towards our goals. Lincoln faced many failures, but he never gave up and eventually became the President of America.

6.2 Thomas Edison

The story of Thomas Edison teaches us that failure is only a learning opportunity. Edison invented the bulb after failing more than 1,000 times. He said, "I haven't failed. I've found 10,000 ways that don't work."

6.3 Mahatma Gandhi

The story of Mahatma Gandhi teaches us that with self-motivation and determination we can achieve our goals. Gandhi brought independence to India through non-violence and Satyagraha.

Leadership and Team Building

Leadership and team building are important for successful network marketing.

1. Inspirational Leadership: Be an inspirational leader. Keep your team motivated and supported.

2.Cooperation and Support: Collaborate with your team members and provide them support. Solve their problems and recognize their achievements.

3.Team Development: Focus on the development and education of your team members. Provide them opportunities to acquire new skills and knowledge.**Self-motivation and dedication**

Self-motivation and dedication are essential for success in network marketing.

1.Self-Motivation: Identify and maintain your sources of inspiration. Remember your objectives and goals.

2.Dedication: Have full dedication towards your business. Keep trying despite difficulties and failures.

3.Self-discipline: Follow self-discipline. Use your time and resources properly.

success stories

Example 1: Mr. Ajay Kumar

Mr. Ajay Kumar achieved extraordinary success in network marketing on the strength of his self-confidence and positive mindset. He regularly attended training programs and built strong relationships with his team. His leadership abilities and dedication made him an inspirational leader.

Example 2: Mrs. Kavita Singh

Mrs. Kavita Singh took her network marketing business to the heights of success with clear goals and a solid plan. They focused on their self-development and built strong relationships with their network members. His self-motivation and dedication made him a successful network marketer.

conclusion

The right mindset and approach are essential to achieving success in network marketing. Positive mindset, self-development, goal setting, networking, leadership, and self-motivation are the keys to your success in network marketing. In this chapter, we discussed these important elements in detail.

Phase-02

Network Marketing now with Artificial Intelligence

[Chapters 11-15]

Chapter 11

Lead Generation and Management

Chapter Introduction

Lead generation is a vital process for any business, especially in direct sales. This process focuses on identifying potential customers and collecting information about them. AI (Artificial Intelligence) can make this process more efficient and effective. Here's how AI impacts lead generation:

Use of AI:

Data Analysis

AI algorithms can analyze data from a variety of sources, such as social media, website traffic, and other online activities. This data helps in understanding the behavior and interests of potential customers.

Profiling

Profiles of potential customers can be created using AI technology. This includes their demographics, preferences, and past purchasing patterns. This allows for more targeted marketing.

Automated Tools

There are many AI based tools available that can generate leads automatically. These tools analyze customer data and identify high-probability leads.

Lead Scoring

In the lead scoring process, AI assigns potential customers a score that reflects their potential value and likelihood of purchasing. This process helps sellers identify which leads should be addressed first.

Benefits of Lead Scoring:

1.Prioritization

By prioritizing leads with higher scores, sellers can make better use of their time and resources.

2.Better Conversion Rates

Focusing on high-quality leads increases conversion rates, because these leads are already interested in the product or service.

3.Resource Saving

Time and effort are not wasted on low-probability leads, which saves resources.

AI Tools and Technologies

Many advanced tools and techniques can be used in AI lead generation and management:

01.Chatbots

Chatbots can automatically83 interact with website visitors and collect information from them. They can also instantly transfer leads to the customer service or sales team.

02. CRM Software

Many CRM software come with AI capabilities that can automate lead scoring and lead management. For example, Salesforce and HubSpot have AI-based lead scoring features.

03. Email Marketing Automation

AI-based email marketing tools can run automated and personalized email campaigns by analyzing customer behavior. These campaigns maintain constant contact with potential customers and help convert them into customers.

Lead Management

In the lead management process, the leads received are effectively managed and nurtured so that they can eventually be converted into customers. AI can make this process even more efficient.

Steps of Lead Management:

01 Lead Capture

Collecting leads information from various sources. This includes website forms, social media, email, and other digital platforms.

02. Lead Qualification

Qualifying Leads Using AI. This process helps to score leads and identify high quality leads.

03. Lead Nurturing

Sending relevant information and content to leads periodically using AI based tools. This makes them loyal to the brand and ready to purchase.

04. Lead Tracking

AI is used to track all interactions with leads. This helps sellers understand what stage leads are in and how to nurture them further.

How to reach people with the help of AI in direct selling business

In direct selling business, reaching out to people and making them aware of your products or services is the key to success. Artificial Intelligence (AI) can make this process more effective and efficient. Here are discussed some of the ways through which you can reach out to people with the help of AI in direct selling business:

1. Social Media Targeting

AI algorithms can be used to reach the right target audience on social media platforms. AI can understand the demographics, interests, and behavior of your ideal customers and create precise ad campaigns based on them.

- **Lookalike Audience**: AI tools can analyze your existing customer list and identify people who resemble your best customers. These lookalike audiences are more likely to be interested in your products or services.
- **sentiment analysis**: AI can monitor discussions about brands and products on social media using sentiment analysis and understand what people think about your products.

2. Email Marketing Automation

Using AI based email marketing tools you can conduct personalized and targeted email campaigns.

- **personalized content**: AI can create personalized email content based on consumer behavior, past purchase history, and interests.
- **Automated Follow-up**: AI can track your email campaigns and send automated follow-up messages. This process can help potential customers in their purchasing decision.

3. Chatbots and Virtual Assistants

Using chatbots and virtual assistants you can provide 24/7 customer support on your website and social media platforms.

- **lead generation**: Chatbots can interact with potential customers, answer their questions, and recommend the right products as per their needs. In the process, they may collect contact information of potential customers.
- **immediate assistance**: Virtual assistants can help customers through the purchasing process by quickly answering their questions.

4. Content Marketing Automation

AI can be used to optimize content marketing campaigns.

- **content curation**: Using AI algorithms, you can identify and present relevant and valuable content to your target audience.
- **Content Distribution**:AI tools can help you post your content on the right platform at the right time, increasing your reach and engagement.

5. Voice Search Optimization

AI can also optimize the use of voice assistants such as Alexa and Google Assistant. With the increasing popularity of voice search, it is important that your content and website are optimized for voice search.

- **Voice-friendly content**: Create content optimized for voice search, including long-tail keywords and use of common language.
- **Voice Assistant Integration**: Integrate your services and products with voice assistants so that potential customers can easily find information about you.

6. Personalized Web Experience

AI tools can be used to provide a personalized experience to visitors to your website.

- **dynamic content**:AI can show dynamic content based on the behavior and preferences of your website visitors.
- **recommendation engine**: AI based recommendation engines can provide product recommendations to your customers based on their interests.

7. Remarketing

AI can be used to optimize remarketing campaigns.

- **personalized advertising**: AI can show personalized ads to customers who have previously visited your website but not made a purchase.
- **consumer behavior analysis**: AI algorithms analyze consumers' behavior and make their purchases.

  Can understand the habits of users and optimize ad campaigns based on them.

Conclusion

Lead generation and management processes can be automated and efficient with the use of AI. It not only helps in generating high quality leads but also manages and nurtures them effectively. As a result, sellers can experience higher conversion rates and increased sales. The use of AI in direct selling could prove to be a game-changer, allowing businesses to grow faster.

Chapter 12

Customer Analytics and Behavioral Analysis

Chapter Introduction

Customer Analytics and Behavioral Analysis play an important role in modern business strategies. In

Direct Selling, these techniques are used to understand customer preferences, needs and buying patterns by analyzing data. AI (Artificial Intelligence) and machine learning make these processes more effective and efficient.

Customer Analytics

1. Data Collection

source: Data collection for customer analytics is done from a variety of sources, such as website analytics, social media, email marketing, and customer surveys.

data type: This includes demographic data, transaction data, and customer interaction data.

2. Data Analysis

AI Algorithm: AI based algorithms can analyze large data sets and provide important insights.

Visualization Tools: Various visualization tools are used to understand the data, such as dashboards and charts.

3. Customer Segmentation

Demographic segmentation: Segmenting customers based on their age, gender, location etc.

Behavioral segmentation: Categorizing customers based on their purchasing behavior and preferences.

Behavioral Analysis

1. Customer Journey Mapping

Stages: The customer journey is divided into different stages, such as awareness, consideration, decision, and loyalty.

Touchpoints: Customer touchpoints are analyzed at each stage.

2. Purchase Pattern Analysis

past purchase data: Future behavior of customers is predicted by analyzing their past purchases.

Recommendation System: AI based recommendation system recommends products to customers based on their past behavior.

3. Customer Behavior Modeling

Predictive Analytics: Future behavior of customers is predicted using AI and machine learning.

Lifetime Value (LTV): The lifetime value of each customer is analyzed so that they can be served in the best way.

Use of AI and Machine Learning

1. Pattern Recognition

Data Mining: AI algorithms recognize patterns and trends in large data sets.

Clustering: Customers are grouped on the basis of their behavior and preferences.

2. Real-Time Analysis

Real-Time Data Processing: AI is used for data processing and analysis in real time.

Immediate Decision: Real-time insights are used to make quick and informed decisions.

3. Personalized Experience

Customized Marketing: AI creates personalized marketing campaigns that are tailored to customers' specific needs and preferences.

Predictive Offers: Special offers and promotions are provided to customers based on their likely purchasing patterns

Business Benefits

1. Increase in Conversion Rates

Targeted Marketing: Converting high quality leads into customers through targeted marketing campaigns.

Better Customer Experience: Increase customer satisfaction and loyalty by providing personalized and relevant experiences.

2. Customer Retention

Loyalty program: Special programs and offers to retain customers and increase their loyalty.

customer feedback: Analysis of customer feedback and improvement measures.

3. Operational Efficiency

Automation: Automating various marketing and sales processes using AI based tools.

Cost Reduction: Reduction in operating costs by increasing efficiency and reducing unnecessary expenses.

Conclusion

Through customer analytics and behavioral analysis, direct selling businesses can not only gain a better understanding of customers but also provide them with personalized and relevant experiences. The use of AI and machine learning technologies can make this process even more efficient and effective, allowing businesses to achieve higher conversion rates, better customer retention, and operational efficiencies. All these factors together contribute significantly to the success and growth of business.

Chapter
13

Predictive Analytics and Sales Forecasting

Chapter Introduction

Predictive Analytics and Sales Forecasting play an important role in the strategic planning and decision making processes of business. These techniques help predict future events and trends using historical data and AI (Artificial Intelligence). In direct selling, predictive analytics enables sellers to more effectively understand the needs of their customers and optimize their sales strategies.

1. Introduction to Predictive Analytics

1.1 What is Predictive Analytics?

Predictive analytics is the process of predicting future outcomes using data, statistical algorithms, and machine learning techniques. It analyzes current and historical data to forecast possible future trends and events.

1.2 Key Components of Predictive Analytics

- **Data Collection:** Collecting data from a variety of sources, such as sales records, customer interactions, and market trends.

- **Data Preprocessing:** Cleaning, formatting, and preparing data for analysis.

- **Model Building:** Building and training machine learning and statistical models.

-**Evaluation of Results:** Evaluating model performance and checking its accuracy.

2. Introduction to Sales Forecasting

2.1 What is sales forecasting?

Sales forecasting is a process in which future sales are predicted by analyzing historical sales data. It helps businesses plan their demand and supply, optimize inventory management, and prepare financial plans.

2.2 Major components of sales forecasting

- **Historical Data:** Use of past sales data.

- **Trend Analysis:** Analysis of long-term sales trends.

- **Seasonality:** Be mindful of seasonal effects.

- **External Factors:** Market trends, competition, and economic conditions.

3. Benefits of Predictive Analytics and Sales Forecasting

3.1 Better decision making process

Predictive analytics and sales forecasting help sellers make informed and data-driven decisions, strengthening their strategic planning.

3.2 Optimized Inventory Management

By using these techniques businesses can forecast their inventory needs more accurately, thereby avoiding stock shortages and excess stock problems.

3.3 Improving customer satisfaction

By anticipating customer needs and preferences, sellers can provide more relevant and timely products and services, thereby increasing customer satisfaction.

4. Use of AI for predictive analytics and sales forecasting

4.1 Machine Learning Models

Machine learning algorithms, such as regression, time series forecasting, and clustering, are used in predictive analytics. These models predict future events by analyzing historical data.

4.2 Natural Language Processing (NLP)

NLP techniques help predict customer sentiments and attitudes by analyzing social media, customer reviews, and other text data.

4.3 Big Data Analytics

Big data technologies enable the analysis of large and diverse data sets, making more accurate and detailed predictions possible.

5. Case Study: Using Predictive Analytics and Sales Forecasting

5.1 Example

- **Company A:** Company A developed a predictive analytics model using its historical sales data and market trends. This model helped them accurately forecast future demand and optimize their inventory management.

- **Company B:** Company B analyzed the purchasing patterns of its customers using machine learning algorithms. This analysis enabled them to run personalized marketing campaigns that significantly increased their sales.

6. Challenges of Predictive Analytics and Sales Forecasting

6.1 Data quality and authenticity

The success of predictive analytics depends on the quality of the data. Poor quality data can lead to incorrect conclusions and predictions.

6.2 Model accuracy

Model accuracy is important. Incorrect modeling techniques or insufficient data can lead to reduced accuracy.

6.3 Data Security and Privacy

Customer data should remain secure and confidential. Maintaining data security and privacy is a significant challenge.

7. Future Trends of Predictive Analytics and Sales Forecasting

7.1 Advanced Machine Learning Techniques

In the future, more advanced machine learning techniques will be developed that will make predictive analytics and sales forecasting even more accurate.

7.2 Real-Time Analytics

Real-time data processing and analytics technologies will enable sellers to make quick decisions and adapt to rapidly changing market conditions.

7.3 Integrated Platforms

Integrated analytics platforms will help sellers bring together different data sources and analyze from a holistic perspective.

closing

Predictive analytics and sales forecasting are important tools to achieve success in direct selling business. By using AI and machine learning technologies, sellers can develop more effective strategies, serve customers better, and steer their businesses toward sustainability and growth. Correct and strategic use of these technologies can enhance the competitiveness of businesses and prepare them for future trends.

Chapter
14

Chatbots and Virtual Assistants

Chapter Introduction

Chatbots and Virtual Assistants are based on Artificial Intelligence (AI) and Machine Learning (ML) technologies to help businesses communicate with customers, solve their problems, and provide services. In direct selling, these technologies enable sellers to connect with their customers in a more effective and efficient manner.

1. Introduction to Chatbots

1.1 What are Chatbots?

Chatbots are AI-powered programs that interact with customers by mimicking human dialogue. They answer customer questions and solve problems using natural language processing (NLP).

1.2 Types of Chatbots

- **Rule-Based Chatbots:**These chatbots work based on predefined rules and answers.

- **AI-Based Chatbots:** These chatbots learn and communicate automatically using machine learning and NLP.

2. Introduction to Virtual Assistants

2.1 What are Virtual Assistants?

Virtual assistants are AI-based programs that act as personal assistants. They automate various tasks, such as setting reminders, email management, and customer service.

2.2 Benefits of Virtual Assistants

- **Personal Service:** Virtual assistants provide personalized and relevant service to customers.

- **Time Saving:** These assistants save sellers time and enable them to focus on more important tasks.

3. Ways to Use Chatbots and Virtual Assistants in Network Marketing

Network marketing is a rapidly growing field in which the use of technological innovations can help businesses grow and establish better communication with customers. Chatbots and virtual assistants are an important part of these innovations, providing many benefits in network marketing. Here we will discuss different ways of using these tools in network marketing.

1. Customer Support

The most common use of chatbots and virtual assistants can be for customer support. They are available 24/7 and able to quickly respond to common customer queries. For example, questions about product information, order status, or the return process can be answered automatically by chatbots.

2. Lead Generation and Qualification

The importance of leads (unfavorable customers) is very high in network marketing. Chatbots can be used to interactively engage website visitors and collect contact information from them. Additionally, these bots can ask a few questions to understand the preferences and needs of potential customers, making qualified leads easier to identify.

3.Personalized Recommendations

Virtual assistants can provide personalized product recommendations based on customers' past purchase history and their behavior. This feature improves customer experience and helps increase sales. For example, a virtual assistant can inform a customer about new products based on their preferences, helping them find the exact product they are looking to purchase.

4. Sales Training and Support

Training new members is an important task in network marketing. Virtual assistants can be used to provide various training modules and materials to new members. Additionally, virtual assistants can be available to immediately answer questions and provide advice, helping new members learn faster and achieve success.

5. Follow-Up and Remarketing

Follow-up is an important process in network marketing, but it can also be time-consuming. Chatbots can be used to send follow-up messages automatically. They can inform customers about offers, discounts, or new products from time to time. Additionally, virtual assistants can be used in remarketing campaigns, reminding customers of products based on their previous searches and purchases.

6. Seamless Shopping Experience

Chatbots can be used to simplify and streamline the process from product selection to purchasing for customers. Chatbots can help customers find the right products, add them to the cart, and even assist with the payment process. This way, customers get a seamless and consistent shopping experience, which increases their satisfaction and trust.

7. Optimizing Marketing Campaigns

Data obtained from chatbots and virtual assistants can be used to optimize marketing campaigns. From the information collected through these tools, businesses can learn which products and offers are most attractive, what times lead to best follow-up, and what type of communication with customers is most effective. This can make marketing campaigns more targeted and effective.

8. Enhancing Customer Experience

Chatbots and virtual assistants can also be used to improve the customer experience. They can be vital in solving customer problems quickly, providing information about products, and keeping them updated from time to time. Better customer experience increases customer loyalty and increases the success of a network marketing business.

9. Automated Webinars and Virtual Events

Webinars and virtual events can be an effective tool in network marketing. Virtual assistants can be used to conduct automated webinars and interact with participants. They can answer questions during events, provide needed materials, and follow-up after the event.

10. Customized Content Delivery

In network marketing, it is important to provide the right information at the right time. Virtual assistants can be used for customized content delivery to customers. They can send customers the right content, such as blog posts, videos, or case studies, based on their profile and behavior to maximize their engagement and engagement.

Chatbots and virtual assistants can bring a big change in network marketing. They not only help in establishing better communication with customers but also enhance the efficiency of the business. Using them, businesses can save time, reduce costs, and establish stronger relationships with customers. As network marketing continues to evolve, the right use of chatbots and virtual assistants can give businesses a competitive edge.

4. Technologies of Chatbots and Virtual Assistants

4.1 Natural Language Processing (NLP)

NLP enables chatbots and virtual assistants to understand and respond to human language. This technology helps them to answer customer queries accurately.

4.2 Machine Learning

Machine learning enables chatbots and virtual assistants to learn and improve their performance based on data. This makes them more effective over time.

4.3 Integration

Chatbots and virtual assistants can be integrated with various platforms and systems, such as CRM systems, social media platforms, and websites.

5. Business Benefits of Chatbots and Virtual Assistants

5.1 Cost Reduction

Chatbots and virtual assistants handle many tasks automatically, reducing the need for human resources and reducing costs.

5.2 Increase in Efficiency

These technologies enable salespeople to work more efficiently, increasing their productivity.

5.3 Improvement in Customer Satisfaction

By providing fast and accurate answers, chatbots and virtual assistants improve customer satisfaction.

I

7. Challenges and Solutions

7.1 Limitations of Chatbots

The capabilities of chatbots may be limited when they encounter complex or unexpected questions. This challenge can be solved through continuous improvements in NLP and machine learning.

7.2 Privacy and Security

Ensuring the security and privacy of customer data is a significant challenge. This problem can be solved by the use of data encryption and security measures.

7.3 Need for human interaction

Some customers prefer human interaction. This challenge can be solved by the use of hybrid systems, where chatbots and human assistants work together.

8. Future trends

8.1 Advanced NLP Techniques

In the future, NLP techniques will be further improved, making chatbots and virtual assistants even more effective.

8.2 Integrated AI Systems

Integrated AI systems will enable sellers to work in better coordination with different platforms and devices.

8.3 Real Time Analysis

Real-time data processing and analysis technologies will enable chatbots and virtual assistants to provide quick and accurate answers.

closing

Chatbots and virtual assistants are revolutionizing the direct selling business. These technologies not only help sellers work more efficiently and effectively, but also provide better service and experience to customers. In the future, the use of these technologies will become even more widespread and advanced, thereby increasing the competitiveness and success of business.

Chapter
15

marketing automation

Chapter Introduction

Marketing automation is a technical process that helps automate marketing campaigns and tasks. It enables businesses to achieve their marketing goals more efficiently and effectively while saving time and resources. In direct selling, marketing automation helps sellers reach customers through personalized, timely and relevant marketing messages.

1. Introduction to Marketing Automation

1.1 What is Marketing Automation?

Marketing automation is the use of software and technologies that help automate, track, and measure various marketing tasks. This includes tasks like email marketing, social media posts, lead generation, and customer relationship management (CRM).

1.2 Key Components of Marketing Automation

- **Email Marketing Automation:** Automated email campaigns that are sent based on customer behavior and preferences.

- **Lead Generation and Nurturing:** Identifying, tracking, and converting potential customers into qualified leads.

- **Social Media Automation:** Automated social media posting and analytics.

- **CRM Integration:** Tracking and managing customer data and interactions.

2. Benefits of Marketing Automation

2.1 Saving time and resources

Marketing automation automatically handles many repetitive tasks, saving time and human resources.

2.2 Personal Marketing

Automation software creates personalized and relevant marketing messages by analyzing customer data and behavior.

2.3 Lead Nurturing and Conversion

Marketing automation tracks potential customers and helps convert them into qualified leads over time.

2.4 Performance Measurement and Analysis

Automation tools measure the performance of marketing campaigns and provide data-based insights, enabling strategic improvements.

3. Major tools of marketing automation

3.1 HubSpot

HubSpot is a popular marketing automation platform that offers features like email marketing, social media management, and CRM.

3.2 Marketo

Marketo is an advanced automation tool that specializes in lead generation, lead scoring, and campaign management.

3.3 Mailchimp

Mailchimp is a leading email marketing automation software suitable for small and large businesses.

4. Marketing Automation Process

4.1 Data collection and management

Collecting, managing, and analyzing customer data to make marketing campaigns personalized and relevant.

4.2 Campaign Planning and Execution

Planning and implementing automated campaigns, such as email campaigns, social media posting, and lead nurturing strategies.

4.3 Performance Measurement and Improvement

Tracking the performance of campaigns, analyzing results, and improving strategies.

5. Uses of Marketing Automation

5.1 Email Marketing

Automated email series that are sent at different stages of the customer lifecycle, such as welcome emails, promotional emails, and follow-up emails.

5.2 Social Media Marketing

Automated social media posting, trend tracking, and engagement analysis.

5.3 Lead Generation and Nurturing

Lead capture forms, lead scoring, and nurturing campaigns that drive prospects to make purchasing decisions.

5.4 Customer Relationship Management (CRM)

Tracking customer interactions, managing customer data, and providing personalized service.

<u>Marketing Automation Problems and Solutions in Direct Selling</u>

Direct selling is a business model in which products and services are sold directly to consumers, without any intermediaries. This model is based on personal contact and networking, but in the digital age, marketing automation has presented new possibilities and challenges in this area. In this article, we will discuss the major problems of marketing automation in direct selling and their solutions.

Marketing Automation Problems

1. Technical Complexity:

There are many tools and software available for marketing automation, which can be difficult to use. Most direct sellers lack technical knowledge, making it difficult to use these tools effectively.

2. Lack of personal contact:

The biggest advantage of direct selling is personal contact. Marketing automation can lead to a lack of personal touch, making it harder to establish deeper connections with customers.

3. Data Security and Privacy:

A large amount of customer data is collected under marketing automation. Ensuring the security and privacy of this data is a big challenge, especially when the incidence of data leaks and cyber attacks is on the rise.

4. Cost

Advanced marketing automation tools and software can be expensive. It may be difficult for small and medium-sized direct selling businesses to afford these costs.

5. User Training and Support:

Using marketing automation tools effectively requires proper training and support. Most direct selling companies do not have these resources available, due to which the equipment is not utilized to its full capacity.

solutions to problems

1. Simple and User-Friendly Tools:

Direct selling companies should choose simple and user-friendly marketing automation tools. Choose tools that are easy to understand and do not require much technical knowledge.

2. Balance of personal contact:

It's important to maintain a personal touch when using marketing automation. For this, automation tools can be used to automate routine communications with customers instead of sending them personalized messages.

3. Data Security Measures:

It is necessary to adopt advanced security measures for data protection. Make sure your marketing automation software has strong encryption and security protocols. Furthermore, it is also important to perform regular data backups and security audits.

4. Cost Management:

Look for cost-effective options for small and medium-sized businesses. Many marketing automation tools offer free or low-cost versions. Also, select only the features that are really essential to your business.

5. User Training and Support:

Direct selling companies should organize regular training sessions for their employees. Also, make a solid plan to get support and resources from the equipment provider.

6. Feedback and Continuous Improvement:

Seek regular feedback and continually improve your strategies to ensure marketing automation success. Improve your automation processes using feedback from customers and team members.

Benefits of Marketing Automation for Successful Direct Selling

1. Time Saving:

Marketing automation automates repetitive tasks like sending emails, posting social media, and analyzing customer data, saving time and allowing more focus to be placed on business.

2. Personal experience:

Through automation, personalized and timely messages can be sent to customers. This strengthens personal relationships with customers and allows services to be tailored to their needs.

3. Better Data Analytics:

Marketing automation tools make it easier to analyze the data collected, helping businesses understand customer habits and preferences. This data is helpful in improving business strategies.

4. Increase in Productivity:

Automation reduces the need for manual tasks, thereby increasing team productivity. Employees can focus on more important tasks, increasing the overall efficiency of the business.

5. Optimization of Marketing Strategies:

Marketing automation makes it easy to track the success of marketing campaigns. This allows you to know which strategies are working and which are not, and adapt your strategies accordingly.

8. Future trends

8.1 AI and Machine Learning

AI and machine learning technologies are making marketing automation smarter and efficient, making more relevant and effective campaigns possible in the future.

8.2 Omni-channel marketing

In the future, omni-channel marketing automation will enable sellers to run integrated and consistent campaigns across different channels.

8.3 Real-Time Analytics

Real-time data processing and analytics techniques will help in instantly measuring and improving the performance of marketing campaigns.

Precautions in Marketing Automation

Marketing automation is a powerful tool that helps businesses automate and effectively manage their marketing activities. However, it is important to take some precautions while using it so that you can take full advantage of its benefits and avoid any possible problems. Here are some important precautions:

1. Data Privacy and Security

- **data security**: Make sure your automation platform follows strong data security measures. Take care of the security of personal information.

- **Privacy Policies**: Provide your customers with clear information about the use of their data and follow privacy policies.

2. Right target audience

- **targeting accuracy**: Make sure your automation tools are reaching the right target audience. Having the wrong target audience can cause your efforts to fail.
- **save and analyze**: Accurately save and analyze customer data so you can deliver the right content and offers based on their behavior and preferences.

3. Relevance and Personalization

- **customized content**: Make content personal and relevant when using automation. Avoid generic content that doesn't appeal to your audience.
- **message accuracy**: Make sure your messages and offers reach the right people at the right time and resonate with customers.

4. Regular monitoring and updates

- **Supervision**: Regularly monitor your automation campaigns and evaluate their effectiveness.
- **Updates and improvements**: Update and improve your automation system according to technical issues and changing marketing trends.

5. Avoid excessive automation

- **human touch**: Avoid excessive automation, as it can deprive customers of the human touch. Try to maintain personal relationships.
- **balance**: Maintain a balance between automation and personal interactions so as not to impact your customer experience.

6. Consistency and Branding

- **Brand Consistency**: Make sure to maintain brand consistency across your automation campaigns. All messaging and content should be consistent with your brand's tone and image.
- **brand voice**: Maintain the brand voice and tone so that customers have a consistent brand experience.

7. Timeliness of message

- **spread over time**: Make sure messages and offers from your automation campaigns are sent on time and match customer actions and behavior.
- **Seasonal and events**: Customize automation campaigns for special occasions and seasonal events to make them more effective.

8. Customer Feedback and Feedback

- **gathering feedback**: Get regular feedback from your customers and use it to improve automation campaigns.
- **solutions and improvements**: Address customer issues and suggestions and

incorporate them into your automation process.

9. Testing and Tracking

- **A/B testing**: A/B test different automation campaigns and messages so you can identify the most effective strategies.
- **results tracking**: Track the results of campaigns and analyze data to improve performance.

conclusion

To take full advantage of the benefits of marketing automation, it is important to take precautions. By paying attention to aspects like data privacy, right target audience, relevance, monitoring, and balance, you can make your automation campaigns more effective and provide a better experience to customers. By keeping these precautions in mind, you can make your marketing automation more successful and effective.

closing

Marketing automation can prove to be an important tool in direct selling, if used correctly. Although there are many challenges before it, these problems can be solved by adopting the right strategies and measures. Taking steps like selecting simple and user-friendly tools, balancing personal touch, data security measures, cost management, user training and support, and continuous improvement can help direct selling businesses take full advantage of marketing automation. Along with this, benefits like time savings, personalized experience, better data analytics, increased productivity, and optimization of marketing strategies can also be achieved. The right use of marketing automation can take direct selling businesses to new heights, allowing them to provide better services to their customers and maintain their competitive edge in the market. Marketing automation is revolutionizing the direct selling business. This technology not only helps sellers work more efficiently and effectively, but also provides better service and experience to customers. In the future, the use of marketing automation will become even more widespread and advanced, increasing the competitiveness and success of businesses.

Specific ;

Important changes in direct selling industry in India

There have been many significant changes in the direct selling industry in India in the last five years. These changes are making this industry more structured, organized and consumer-friendly. Some of the major changes are described below

1. Rules and Regulations

Direct Selling and Consumer Protection Act, 2019

Direct selling is a business model in which products and services are sold directly to consumers, without any intermediaries or retail outlets. With the increasing popularity of this business model, the need for protection of consumer rights and monitoring of business practices has also increased. Keeping this in mind, the Government of India enacted **Consumer Protection Act, 2019**, in which clear guidelines and rules have been made for direct selling also.

Introduction to Consumer Protection Act, 2019

The Consumer Protection Act, 2019 has been enacted with the objective of protecting the rights of consumers. This act provides legal protection to consumers to protect them from trade practices, unfair contracts, and other related issues. The Act provides various rights to consumers, such as complaints about defective goods, protection from unfair trade practices, and protection from misrepresentations in advertising.

Guidelines for Direct Selling

Under the Consumer Protection Act, 2019, several guidelines have been issued to regulate direct selling. These guidelines are mandatory for both direct selling companies and their distributors. Following are some key guidelines:

1.Registration and Regulation: Direct selling companies are required to register their business in India. They have to register all their distributors' information and business model with the government.

2.Ethical Business Practices: Direct selling companies and distributors must follow ethical business practices. They should provide accurate and transparent information about goods and services to consumers.

3. Non-Fraud Contract: Contracts between direct selling companies and consumers must be fair and non-fraudulent. All terms and conditions should be clearly mentioned in the contract.

4. Return and Refund Policy: There should be a clear return and refund policy for consumers. If the consumer is not satisfied with a product, he or she should have the right to return the product within a specified time frame and receive a refund.

5. Proper Advertisement: Advertisements should provide correct information about products and services. Action can be taken against companies for making false or misleading advertisements.

6. Consumer Grievance Redressal: Direct selling companies should establish an effective mechanism for redressal of consumer complaints. Consumers can lodge their complaints and should receive timely resolution.

7. Financial Transparency: Distributors should be given clear information about their income and commission. Hiding any financial information or giving wrong information can lead to legal action.

Consumer rights for direct selling

Under the Consumer Protection Act, 2019, direct selling provides the following rights to consumers:

1. Right to Safe Products: Consumers have the right to receive safe and defect-free products. If a product is found to be defective, consumers have the right to return or exchange it.

2. Right to factual information: The consumer has the right to get correct information about the product and service. Companies should share all necessary information with consumers, including product quality, price, and return policy.

3. Right to Choose: Consumers have the right to choose from various options. They should have freedom to choose products without pressure or fraud.

4. Right to Complain: The consumer has the right to complain about any unfair trade practice or lack of service. For this, an effective grievance redressal system has been established.

5. Right to Justice: The consumer has the right to seek justice for violation of his rights. Consumer Dispute Redressal Commissions have been constituted, where consumers can register their complaints.

Necessary steps for direct selling companies

Direct selling companies should take the following steps to ensure compliance with the guidelines of the Consumer Protection Act, 2019:

1. Consumer Education: Organize awareness programs to educate consumers about their rights. Provide them with complete information about the products and services.

2. Legal Compliance: Ensure compliance with all legal and regulatory requirements. Make your business model, contracts, and advertising compliant with the law.

3. Adherence to Good Business Practices: Follow ethical business practices and deal with consumers transparently. Adhere to the highest standards to maintain trust and credibility with customers.

4. Grievance Redressal System: Establish a strong grievance redressal system, so that consumer complaints can be resolved quickly and effectively.

5. Training of distributors: Train your distributors about the Consumer Protection Act, so that they can treat consumers properly and follow company policies.

The Consumer Protection Act, 2019 has provided a structured and regulated environment for the direct selling industry. This act ensures the protection of consumer rights and encourages direct selling companies to make their business practices ethical and transparent. By adopting the right compliance and consumer centric approach, direct selling companies can not only avoid legal risks but also build stronger relationships with their customers, thereby continuing to grow their business.

-Direct Selling Guidelines 2016: The government had issued guidelines for direct selling in 2016, which were incorporated in the Consumer Protection Act of 2019. These have increased transparency and accountability in the industry.

2. Use of digital technology

-Online Platform: Many direct selling companies have increased the use of digital platforms to sell their products and services online. This has provided consumers with an easy and convenient way of shopping.

-Social Media Marketing: The use of social media has increased rapidly. Direct sellers are expanding their network and reaching out to new customers by using Facebook, Instagram, WhatsApp etc.

3. Training and Development

- **E-Learning and Webinars:** Companies have started using e-learning modules and webinars for training. This provides sellers with ongoing training and development opportunities, no matter where they are located.

- **Virtual Meetings:** During the COVID-19 pandemic, virtual meetings and online seminars played an important role. This ensured business continuity and revealed new opportunities.

4. Product Diversity

- Expansion of product range: Direct selling companies have expanded their product range, including health, beauty, home care, personal care, and digital products. This has given consumers more choices and increased market reach.

5. Customer Centric Approach

- **Better customer service**: Companies have started using AI and chatbots to improve customer service. This results in faster resolution of customer problems.

-**Personalization:** Data analytics are being used to provide personalized experiences to customers. This has increased customer satisfaction and trust.

6. Development of industry

- **Organizational change: many** Companies have made changes in their organizational structures, allowing them to become more competitive and innovative.

- **Formation of industry organizations:** Direct selling companies have formed industry organizations, such as IDSA (Indian Direct Selling Association), to help maintain and improve industry standards.

These changes are making the Indian direct selling industry more organized, transparent and consumer-friendly. This is increasing both the credibility and popularity of the industry.

people and public opinion

There have been many significant changes in the perception of people and the public towards the direct selling industry. Unlike earlier negative attitudes, today people consider this industry as a serious and profitable opportunity.

2.1. initial approach

Earlier people's views regarding direct selling were quite negative. It was often considered a scam or pyramid scheme. Many people believed that only the promoters get profit from the people who invest in it and the common distributor gets less profit.

- **Doubt and distrust:** People's distrust and skepticism towards direct selling mainly focused on its legitimacy. It was often seen as "bogus" and "non-transparent".
- **Attractive offer:** Companies used to present their plans as very attractive offers, which made some people feel duped.

2.2. Current situation and changing views

With time, there have been significant changes in people's views. Today direct selling is seen as a potential and profitable career option.

- **Professional Approach:** Today's direct selling companies adopt a more professional approach and maintain transparency. They have improved the business model and become more honest towards customers.
- **Entrepreneurship Opportunity:** People have accepted direct selling as an entrepreneurial opportunity. It is a platform where people can prove their abilities and run their business.
- **Administrative and Legal Reforms:** The government has also implemented new rules and regulations to control this industry, which has increased people's confidence.

Changes in the network marketing industry in India in the next 10 years

The network marketing industry, also known as direct selling or multi-level marketing (MLM), has made significant progress in India over the last few years. Currently, this industry is developing rapidly and may see many important changes in the coming decade. In this article, we will discuss the possible changes that will take place in the network marketing industry in India in the next 10 years.

1. Digital and technological innovation

digital transformation Network marketing will shape the future of the industry. Over the next 10 years, there will be many significant changes in the industry driven by the impact of digital and technological innovations.

1.1. Expansion of online platform

The use of digital marketing and e-commerce platforms will become more common for network marketing companies. Both distributors and customers will use online mediums, thereby increasing the reach and effectiveness of the business.

- **Major role of social media:** Social media platforms such as Facebook, Instagram, and LinkedIn will become important tools for network marketing. These platforms will not only provide marketing opportunities but will also boost brand awareness and customer engagement.
- **Multi-channel marketing:** Companies will promote their products and services through various digital channels, such as email marketing, webinars, and online events.

1.2. Artificial Intelligence (AI) and Data Analytics

The use of AI and data analytics will help improve personalized experience and customization in network marketing.

- **Customer Engagement:** AI chatbots and virtual assistants will make interactions with customers automated and more effective, leading to better customer service and quicker resolutions.

- **Data Driven Decisions:** Companies will use data analytics to predict customer behavior and trends, helping them optimize their marketing campaigns and strategies.

2. Legal and regulatory changes

There is also a possibility of legal and regulatory changes regarding the network marketing industry in India. These changes will affect the practices and standards of the industry.

2.1. Strict rules and regulations

Government and regulatory bodies can impose strict rules and regulations for network marketing companies, to make the industry more transparent and reliable.

- **Transparency:** Companies may be forced to maintain greater transparency about their business models and income distribution. This will reduce potential frauds and schemes.
- **routine inspection:** Regular inspections and audits may be conducted to ensure compliance with rules and regulations.

2.2. Consumer Protection

Strict measures can be taken for consumer protection, so that the safety of customers can be ensured.

- **Consumer Grievance Redressal:** Effective mechanisms can be established to resolve consumer complaints and problems, thereby providing better assistance to customers.

- **Major Certifications:** Network marketing companies may be required to go through a process of certification and licensing to ensure the legality and reliability of their operations.

3. Changes in Market and Competition

Changes may also be seen in the market and competition situation in the future of the network marketing industry.

3.1. market diversity

In the coming years, network marketing companies will introduce a variety of products and services, increasing diversity in the market.

- **innovation:** Companies will introduce new and innovative products that meet specific customer needs and preferences.
- **Regional and local products:** Local and regional products can be introduced through network marketing, allowing customers to take advantage of products near them.

3.2. growth and competition

Competition in the network marketing industry is likely to increase as more companies and new players enter the field.

- **Latest Techniques and Strategies:** Companies will adopt the latest technology and marketing strategies to maintain their competitive advantage.

- **Customer Satisfaction:** Companies will pay special attention to improving customer satisfaction and experience, so that they can retain their customers and increase their loyalty.

4. Social and cultural change

Social and cultural changes may also impact the network marketing industry.

4.1. entrepreneurial spirit

The spirit of entrepreneurship is on the rise in India, and people are looking for independent business and income opportunities. Network marketing can help fulfill this trend.

- **Freedom and Flexibility:** People are looking for greater freedom and flexibility that is possible in network marketing. This can become an attractive career option for young professionals and women.
- **Educational and Vocational Skills:** Education and business skills can be developed in the field of network marketing, giving individuals more knowledge and experience in operating a business.

4.2. Social Impact and Responsibility

The trend to emphasize social responsibility and sustainability can also play an important role in the network marketing industry.

- **Environmental Impact:** Companies will adapt their products and packaging from an environmental perspective and demonstrate their commitment to sustainability.
- **Social Initiative:** Network marketing companies will encourage social initiatives and charity programs to contribute positively to the society.

"In the journey of Direct Selling, every challenge is an opportunity and every failure is a learning experience. The most important mantra to get success in this business is – persistence, patience and positive attitude. Be firm on your goal to make your dreams come true And never let your efforts diminish.

This book has been a companion and guide for you, but remember that the real journey begins now. Maintain your confidence, strengthen your network and always be ready to write your story.

Remember, your success is not just yours, it also belongs to all the people who are inspired by you and join you on this journey. Come, make a fresh start and take your life to new heights through direct selling.Eh.

Go ahead and fly your dreams.

Thanks and best wishes.

epilogue

dear readers,

Through this book "How to Achieve Success with the Help of AI in Direct Selling" you have tried to understand the importance and possibilities of using Artificial Intelligence (AI) in the Direct Selling Industry. At the end of this journey, I, Mukesh Bhati, thank you for sparing your precious time to read this book and imbibe its principles and techniques.

The use of AI in the direct selling industry can prove to be a game-changer. In this book we have discussed various aspects – lead generation, customer management, marketing automation, and data analysis. By using these AI techniques correctly, you can not only increase your productivity and effectiveness, but also provide a more personalized and satisfying customer experience.

future direction

The future of direct selling is even brighter with AI and digital technologies. This book is only a beginning. The continuous innovations and advancements in AI will provide countless opportunities to take your business to new heights. We need to constantly learn and keep pace with changing technologies.

final thoughts

My aim in writing this book was not only to educate you about the importance and usefulness of AI but also to inspire you to get the most out of these technologies by implementing them in your business. I hope this book has given you new vision and new energy.

I would like to remind you that the path to success is always challenging, but with the right direction, the right techniques, and a strong intention, you can achieve any goal. AI is a tool to empower your efforts, but your persistence, dedication, and hard work are the real keys to your success.

thanks and best wishes

Finally, I want to thank you for reading this book and adopting its ideas. I wish you every success and hope you scale new heights in your direct selling business. If you have any questions, suggestions, or feedback, I would look forward to getting in touch with you.

For your success,

Mukesh Bhati